Where raw talent meets real technique—your breakthrough is now

TRADE SECRETS

Foreword(s) from Johnny Whitaker, Lance Britt, and JD Demers.

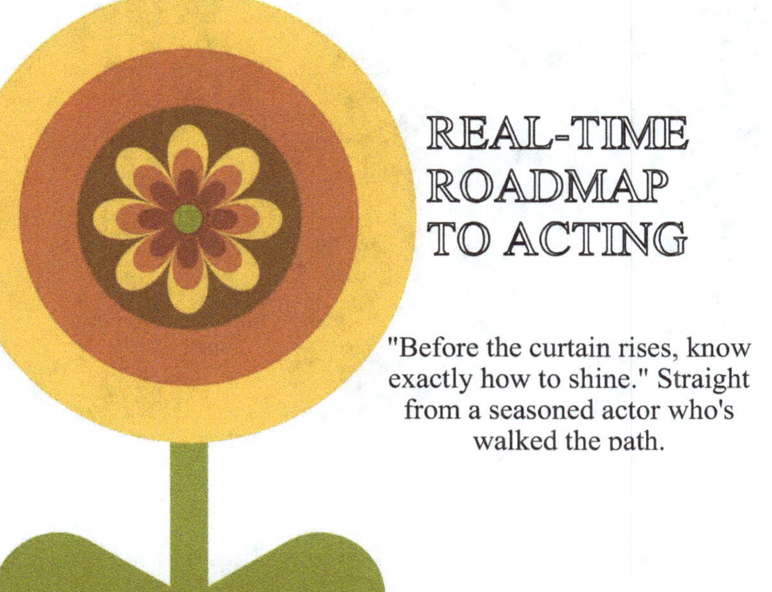

REAL-TIME ROADMAP TO ACTING

"Before the curtain rises, know exactly how to shine." Straight from a seasoned actor who's walked the path.

Catherine Sewell and Grandson Gavan Dowdy.

TRADE SECRETS

CATHERINE SEWELL

*Foreword(s) by Johnny Whitaker,
Lance Britt, and JD Demers.*

REAL-TIME ROADMAP TO ACTING

Published in United States of America

DonnaInk Publications, L.L.C.

Owlhouse Books | Beat Deep Books
Publishing Since 2012
DonnaInk Publications, L.L.C. and Imprints

Library of Congress Cataloging-in-Publication 2022944103.

Sewell, Catherine, author.

TITLE: "TRADE SECRETS: Real-time Roadmap to Acting" / Catherine Sewell.

310 p. cm.

BISAC: BUS043000 – Business & Economics / Careers / Entertainment; BUS109000 Business & Economics / Women in Business; EDU003000 Education / Aims & Objective; EDU029050 Education / Teaching / Subjects / Arts & Humanities; PER001000 – Performing Arts / Acting & Auditioning; PER004000 Performing Arts / Film / General; PER-004010 – Performing Arts / Film / Guides & Reviews; PER004010 Performing Arts / Film / Direction & Production; PER004060 Performing Arts / Film / Genres / General; PER-004110 Performing Arts / Film / Genres / Documentary; PER004160 Performing Arts / Film / Regional & National; PER008000 Performing Arts / Radio / General; PER010000 Performing Arts / Television / General; PER011000 – Performing Arts / Theater / General; PER014000 Performing Arts / Business Aspects; PER023000 Performing Arts / Voice Acting; SEL027000 and SEL-031000 – Self-Help / Personal Growth / Success.

IDENTIFIERS: ISBN – 13 - 978-1-939425-31-7 (alk. color softcover); ISBN – 13 - 978-1-960431-01-1 (alk. color hardback); ISBN – 13 - 978-1-960431-55-4 (alk. b/w softcover); ISBN – 13 - 978-1-960431-54-7 (alk. hardback).

DISCLAIMER: Welcome to this DonnaInk Publications nonfiction edition. These pages reflect real people, events, and places, conveyed through the author's authentic voice and narrative intent. All perspectives are the author's own. Recreated scenes and dialogue arise from personal memory and are presented as such, representing lived experience rather than verbatim transcription. The author assumes no liability for errors or omissions. At DonnaInk, we honor the integrity of nonfiction while recognizing the artistry inherent in personal narrative.

ABOUT THIS TITLE: This title offers an authentic look into the author's acting journey, shaped by real experiences and personal memory. Scenes are interpretive, not verbatim, and all perspectives reflect the author's narrative integrity.

Printed in the United States of America

First Edition: 12 11 10 9 8 7 6 5 4 3 2 1; 2026.

DonnaInk Publications, L.L.C.
17611 Aquasco Road, Brandywine, MD 20613
www.donnaink.net
msdonnalquesinberry@donnaink.net

DEDICATION

A PRECIOUS JOURNEY UNFOLDS

On a sweltering August day in 1969, destiny whispered—a baby boy, wrapped in anticipation, arrived. Our extended family gathered, hearts brimming with joy, to embrace this extraordinary gift. His childhood and teenage years danced with laughter—birthdays, cherished Christmases, church gatherings, and the rhythm of the family dairy farm. Summers meant sandy toes at the beach and countless reunions under the sun.

David, William, and Cecily—siblings bound by love, not rivalry. Their shared pride in each other's accomplishments transcended youth into adulthood. Guided by unwavering faith, their parents, Bill and Carole Summey, instilled values that would shape their lives.

As David matured, he chose to remain rooted in the embrace of his beloved Southern Wesleyan College. His career blossomed where passion met purpose. But it was in volunteering—where he met Andrea Campbell, his soul's counterpart—that David's heart found its true calling. Together, they poured love into helping handicapped children, weaving a tapestry of compassion.

Family remained David's compass. He rarely missed a reunion, except for one—a honeymoon shared with Andrea on a June day in 1995. Their love, like a quiet stream, flowed through the years.

And then, in his unassuming way, David touched lives. His memorial, a gathering of souls, bore witness to a life well-lived.

As he rested beneath the open sky, a single white dove circled—a celestial whisper of eternity.

David's earthly journey may have been brief, but his memory etches permanence in our hearts..

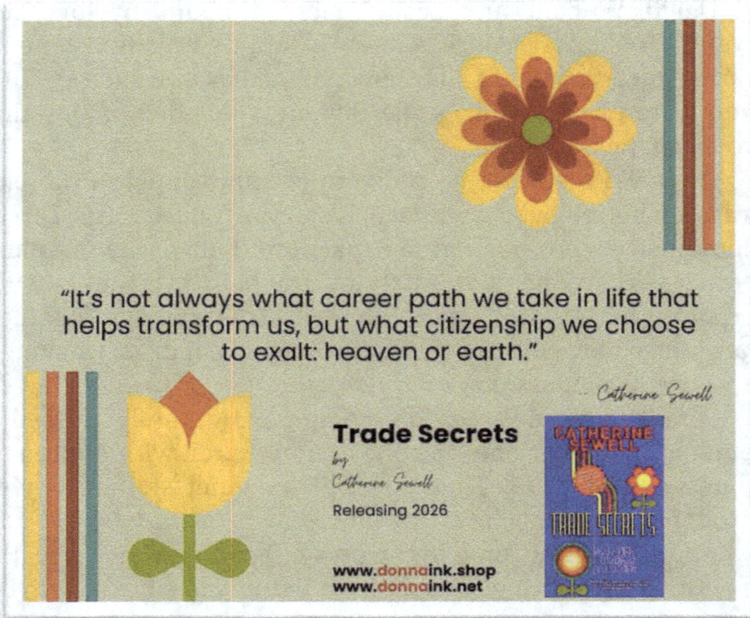

DAVID JOHN SUMMEY

JULY 13, 1969-APRIL 5, 2005

This book is dedicated to David John Summey,
my nephew, who was my biggest fan.
In loving memory of his life,
and many thanks for his love…
and in support of my career.
Thank you, David. I love and miss you.

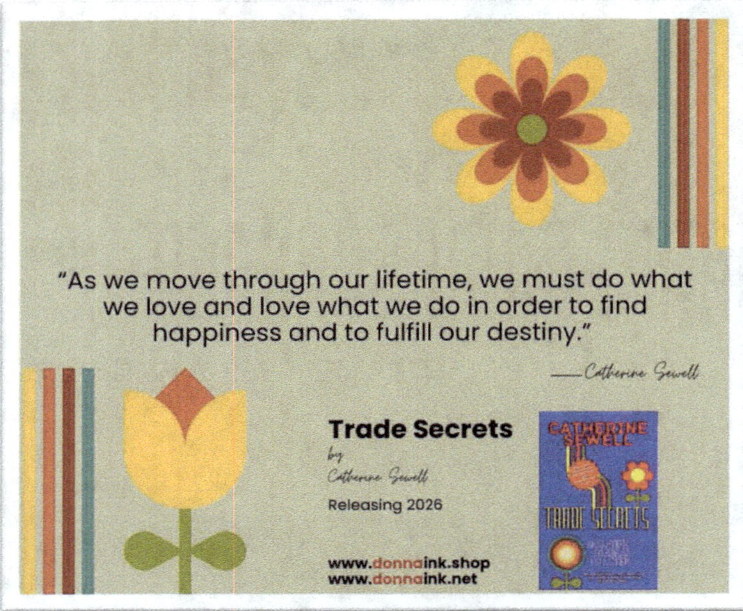
"As we move through our lifetime, we must do what we love and love what we do in order to find happiness and to fulfill our destiny."
—Catherine Sewell
Trade Secrets
by
Catherine Sewell
Releasing 2026
www.donnaink.shop
www.donnaink.net
CATHERINE SEWELL
TRADE SECRETS

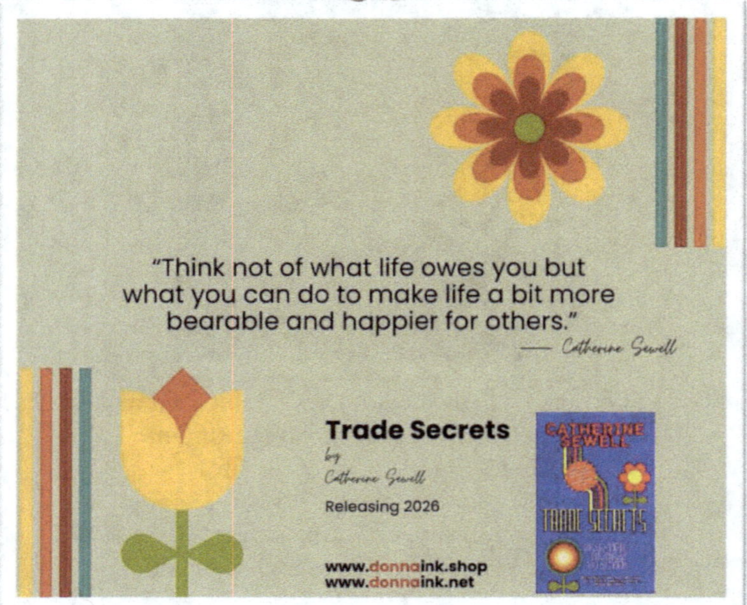
"Think not of what life owes you but what you can do to make life a bit more bearable and happier for others."
— Catherine Sewell
Trade Secrets
by
Catherine Sewell
Releasing 2026
www.donnaink.shop
www.donnaink.net
CATHERINE SEWELL
TRADE SECRETS

EPIGRAPH

ORIGINAL AND CURATED QUOTES SHOWCASED BY CATHERINE SEWELL

"Today, I realize what I want in life is up to me. There is no one in my way. If I want something, I know desire is not enough. I need to do what it takes to be a winner, before I can win."

—Catherine Sewell

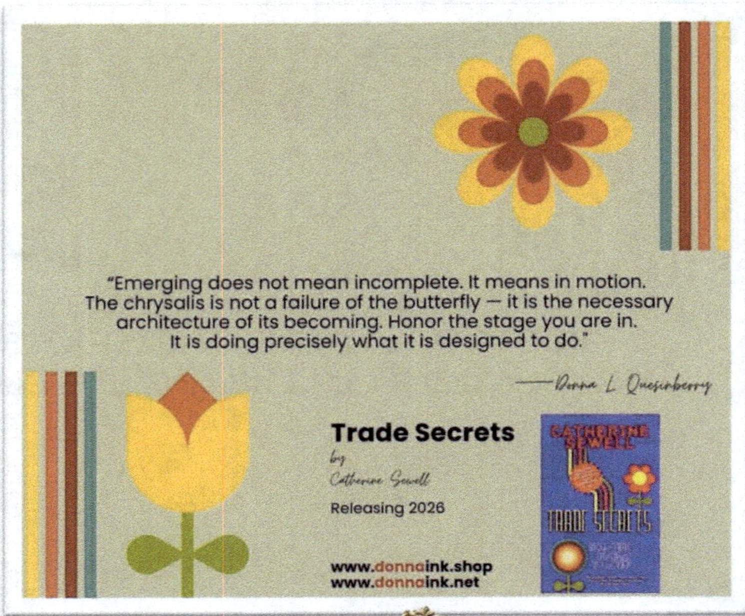
"Emerging does not mean incomplete. It means in motion. The chrysalis is not a failure of the butterfly — it is the necessary architecture of its becoming. Honor the stage you are in. It is doing precisely what it is designed to do."
—Donna L Quesinberry
Trade Secrets
by
Catherine Sewell
Releasing 2026
www.donnaink.shop
www.donnaink.net

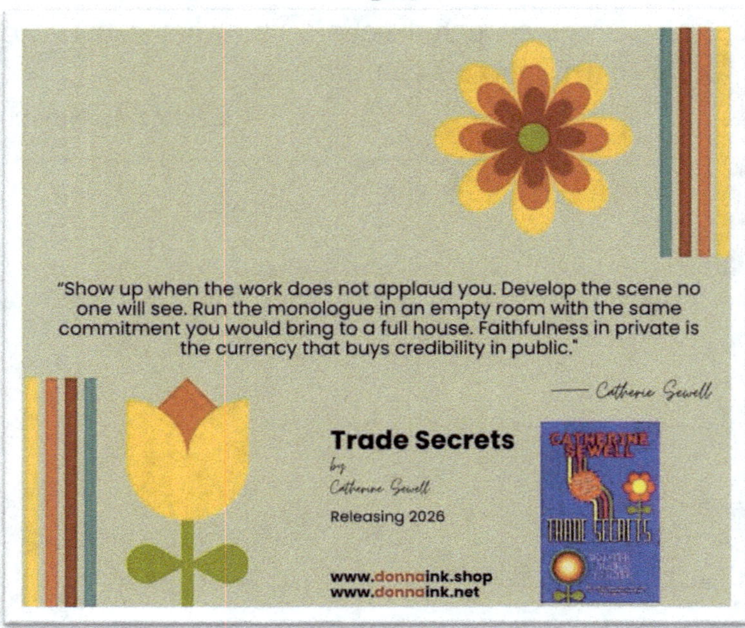
"Show up when the work does not applaud you. Develop the scene no one will see. Run the monologue in an empty room with the same commitment you would bring to a full house. Faithfulness in private is the currency that buys credibility in public."
— Catherine Sewell
Trade Secrets
by
Catherine Sewell
Releasing 2026
www.donnaink.shop
www.donnaink.net

TABLE OF CONTENTS

TRADE SECRETS:
A REAL-TIME ROADMAP TO ACTING

"Every actor who has ever commanded a stage or inhabited a screen began in the exact same place. The beginning is not a disadvantage. It is the only honest place from which anything real ever grows."
—Unknown
Trade Secrets
by
Catherine Sewell
Releasing 2026
www.donnaink.shop
www.donnaink.net
CATHERINE SEWELL
TRADE SECRETS

"The actor's primary instrument is not the voice or the body. It is attention — the sustained, unhurried, compassionate capacity to observe what a human being actually does when something real is happening to them. Study people the way a musician studies sound: as if your entire art depends on getting it right. It does."
— Catherine Sewell
Trade Secrets
by
Catherine Sewell
Releasing 2026
www.donnaink.shop
www.donnaink.net
CATHERINE SEWELL
TRADE SECRETS

FOREWORD INTRO

PERSPECTIVES BEFORE THE CURTAIN RISES

I am honored to open this book with reflections from three industry professionals whose voices and support have shaped my acting in meaningful ways. Each of them has walked beside me at different points in my career, and I hold their respect and camaraderie in the highest regard.

- **Johnny Whitaker**, beloved actor and advocate, offers wisdom from his own journey in entertainment, inspiring those who follow the path he helped shape.
- **Lance Britt**, producer and creative visionary, contributes his perspective on artistry, dedication, and the essential role of community in the performing arts.
- **JD Demers**, writer and industry professional, shares insight into the craft and the resilience it demands.

Together, their words set the stage for what follows. Each Foreword reminds us that an actor's path is never walked alone—it is illuminated by mentors, peers, and fellow travelers who believe in the power of storytelling.

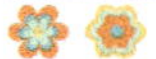

"We are what we repeatedly do.
Excellence, then, is not an act, but a habit."
Trade Secrets
Releasing 2026
www.donnaink.shop
www.donnaink.net

"Nature is an endless combination
and repetition of a very few laws."
Trade Secrets
Releasing 2026
www.donnaink.shop
www.donnaink.net

FOREWORD ONE

JOHNNY WHITAKER

JOHNNY WHITAKER
Tom Sawyer - 1973
Credit: Mr. Whitaker's IMDb

JOHNNY WHITAKER
Sigmund and the Seamonster - 2017
Credit: Mr. Whitaker's IMDb

It is with genuine pleasure and deep respect I offer this Foreword to Catherine Sewell's *TRADE SECRETS: A Real-Time Roadmap to Acting*. Over the years, I've had the privilege of working alongside Catherine on several productions. In that time, I've come to admire not only her talent, but also the heart, discipline, and integrity she brings to every set.

Catherine is an artist who stands out. Her skill is undeniable, but what truly distinguishes her is the way she approaches the craft with humility, curiosity, and a work ethic that speaks for itself. She didn't come into this industry through the traditional channels of drama schools or theatrical lineage. Instead, she carved her own path with resilience, humor, and grace. That journey gives her a perspective that is invaluable to Actors who are still finding their footing.

Her academic background in education and psychology has only strengthened her instincts as a performer. She listens deeply, collaborates generously, and maintains a level of professsionalism that elevates every project she touches. Whether she's arriving early, staying late, or absorbing direction with her characteristic openness, Catherine embodies what it means to be a dedicated student of the craft. Her career — spanning more than one hundred and fifty films, along with work in comercials, theater, and filmmaking — reflects both her versatility and her unwavering commitment.

What I've always appreciated about Catherine is her respect for the work itself. She approaches every role, no matter the size, with the same level of intention and care. She understands that each part contributes to the whole, and she embraces that responsibility with sincerity.

In *Trade Secrets*, Catherine shares her hard-earned wisdom with generosity and clarity. This is not a theoretical book — it's a practical, real-world guide filled with insights Actors can apply immediately. She speaks honestly about the realities of the industry, offering a balanced view that acknowledges both the challenges and the rewards of pursuing this demanding profession.

What impressed me most in our collaborations was Catherine's kindness, professionalism, and relentless desire to grow. She is not only a gifted actress, but a thoughtful and committed learner and that dedication shines through on every page of this book.

TRADE SECRETS is more than a guide; it is a reflection of Catherine's spirit and her desire to uplift others. It will inspire, challenge, and empower aspiring Actors to pursue their dreams with purpose and determination. I wholeheartedly recommend it to anyone serious about building a career in this industry.

I am proud to have worked with Catherine, and I am delighted to see her share her wisdom with the next generation. This book stands as a testament to her talent, perseverance, and generosity of heart.

—Johnny Whitaker

JOHNNY WHITAKER BIOGRAPHY

John Orson Whitaker, Jr. (born December 13, 1959) is an American actor notable for several film and television performances during his childhood. The redheaded Whitaker played Jody Davis on *Family Affair* from 1966 to 1971. He originated the role of Scotty Baldwin on *General Hospital* in 1965, played the lead in Hallmark's 1969 *The Littlest Angel*, and portrayed the title character in the 1973 musical version of *Tom Sawyer*.

Early Life - Whitaker was born in the Los Angeles neighborhood of Van Nuys, the fifth of eight children of Thelma and John O. Whitaker, Sr.

Acting Career - Whitaker began his professional acting career at the age of three by appearing in a television commercial for a local used-car dealer. He went on to appear in advertisements for Mattel Toymakers, for such toys as *Larry the Lion* and *Crackers the Parrot* in their *Animal Yackers* series. In 1965, Whitaker originated the character of the young Scotty Baldwin in the soap opera *General Hospital*. In 1966, he acted in a major feature film, *The Russians Are Coming, The Russians Are Coming*, which starred Brian Keith. After Keith was cast as the lead in the television series *Family Affair*, he recommended Whitaker to play the part of his on-screen nephew.

Family Affair aired from 1966 to 1971. It co-starred Whitaker playing the role of an orphaned boy named Jody Davis, living in a high-rise apartment in New York City with his twin sister Buffy (Anissa Jones) and older sister Cissy (Kathy Garver). His bachelor uncle Bill Davis (Brian Keith); and Bill's gentleman's gentleman, Mr. French (Sebastian Cabot). Jody and Buffy were originally supposed to be different ages, but the show's producers thought Whitaker and Jones looked so cute together that they changed them to be twins.

While still appearing regularly on *Family Affair*, in 1968 Whitaker was a featured guest star (along with Julie Harris) in *A Dream to Dream*, a poignant episode of *Bonanza*, written by series costar Michael Landon.

During breaks in production of *Family Affair*, Whitaker starred in the *Hallmark Hall of Fame* production, *The Littlest Angel*, alongside

Fred Gwynne and Tony Randall, and an episode of the longrunning Western, *The Virginian*, both aired in 1969.

Also, in 1969, Whitaker was a guest star playing Jack in an episode of *Bewitched* titled, *Samantha and the Beanstalk*. In 1970, Whitaker played the part of Willie in a *Green Acres* episode titled, *The Confrontation*. Later, he played Dinky Watson in a *Green Acres* episode titled, *The Beeping Rock*. Later on in 1970, he played the main character of Justin in *The Church of Jesus Christ of Latter-day Saints'* film, *A Day For Justin*.

Whitaker and Scott Kolden on, *Sigmund and the Sea Monsters*, 1973. After *Family Affair*, he appeared in a two-part episode of *Gunsmoke* in 1971. Whitaker went on to star in the 1973 Sid and Marty Krofft Saturday morning children's series, *Sigmund and the Sea Monsters* alongside Billy Barty and Scott Kolden, and appeared in feature films, including Disney's, *Snowball Express* (1972), *The Biscuit Eater* (1972), *Napoleon and Samantha* (1972), and *The Magic Pony* (1977). His most prominent feature film role during this period was the lead in the musical version of *Tom Sawyer* (1973).

In an interview with Tom Snyder on *The Late Late Show*, Whitaker said he had also worked as a computer consultant at CBS. He later joined a Los Angeles talent agency, *Whitaker Entertainment*, owned by his sister. Whitaker also was Dana Plato's Manager.

In 1999, Whitaker received the *Young Artist Former Child Star Lifetime Achievement Award* at the *20th Youth in Film Awards*. In 2012, Whitaker co-produced and co-hosted a short-lived radio talk show, *The Dr. Zod and Johnny Show*. The following year, he appeared onstage in *Judson Theatre Company's* production of *To Kill a Mockingbird* in the cameo role of Judge Taylor. In 2016, Whitaker gave a guest-star cameo appearance in Amazon's reboot of *Sigmund and the Sea Monsters*. In the premiere episode, he played the part of heckling boat owner Zach, against David Arquette's salty character *Captain Barnabas*. The episode had a similar cameo appearance by original show creators Sid and Marty Krofft.

—Credit: Wikipedia

YEAR	TITLE	ROLE	FORMAT
1965	*General Hospital*	Scotty Baldwin	TV Series
1966	*The Russians Are Coming; The Russians Are Coming*	Alex	Film
1966–1971	*Family Affair*	Jody Davis	TV Series
1968	*Bonanza* ("A Dream to Dream")	Guest role	TV Episode
1969	*The Littlest Angel*	The Littlest Angel	TV Film (Hallmark Hall of Fame)
1969	*The Virginian*	Guest role	TV Episode
1969	*Bewitched* ("Samantha and the Beanstalk")	Jack	TV Episode
1970	*Green Acres* ("The Confrontation")	Willie	TV Episode
1970	*Green Acres* ("The Beeping Rock")	Dinky Watson	TV Episode
1972	*Snowball Express*	Richard Baxter	Film
1972	*Napoleon and Samantha*	Napoleon	Film
1972	*The Mystery in Dracula's Castle*	Stevie	TV Film
1973	*Tom Sawyer*	Tom Sawyer	Film (musical)
1973–1975	*Sigmund and the Sea Monsters*	Johnny Stuart	TV Series
1973	*Something Evil*	Stevie	TV Film
1974	*Mulligan's Stew*	Jimmy Mulligan	TV Series
1974	*Mobile One*	Mike	TV Series
1974	*Gunsmoke*	Guest role	TV Episode
1974	*Marcus Welby, M.D.*	Guest role	TV Episode
1977	*The Secrets of Isis*	Guest role	TV Episode
1997	*The New Adventures of Sigmund and the Sea Monsters*	Cameo	TV Special
2013	*A Talking Cat!?!*	Phil	Film
2013	*A Talking Pony!?!*	Horatio (voice)	Film
2014	*Knock 'Em Dead*	Jack (voice)	Film
2016	*A Husband for Christmas*	Santa	TV Movie
2016	*The Wrong Child*	Mr. Haight	TV Movie
2016–2017	*Sigmund and the Sea Monsters* (Amazon reboot)	Zach	TV Series

2019	*The Miss Adventures of Camp Elaine*	Angel Agent	TV Series
2021	*TV Therapy*	Johnny	TV Series
2024	*The Last Evangelist*	Bishop	TV Series

Highlights & Notes

- **Breakout role:** Jody Davis in *Family Affair* (1966–1971).
- **Disney era:** Leading roles in *Napoleon and Samantha* (1972) and *Tom Sawyer* (1973).
- **Cult favorite:** *Sigmund and the Sea Monsters* (1973–1975), later reprised in the 2016 reboot.
- **Later career:** Returned in the 2010s with family films (*A Talking Cat!?!*) and faith-based projects (*The Last Evangelist*).

FOREWORD TWO

LANCE BRITT

LANCE BRITT
Across The Canvas Productions
Credit: IMDb

I am Lance Britt. I founded my record company, *Across the Canvas Productions* in 1978 at which time I had already been in the entertainment industry for over 20 years. In April of 1997, I expanded the entity into an entertainment company to include, Film, Television, Video, Fashion, Art, All Print and Digital Media including the Internet. I began to write articles for Entertainment Journals and post castings on the World Wide Web. I received thousands of headshots and resumes from all over the world. The website would get as many as Seven Million visits a day. Among these responses to the castings were submissions from Sherman Carmichael's talents.

Bruce Williamson, Noël Baker, Marty Richardson, and Catherine Sewell were among the first individuals to appear in our productions. Catherine became Host and Tour Guide for our numerous programs, where she would interview people in the entertainment industry and others from around the world.

She was a natural with her background as an educator and her personal demeanor. She connected with the guests as if they had been lifelong friends. In January 2000, *Blank Surfaces* went into production. Catherine was Host for segments done on the East Coast. Todd Johnson was the Host for productions done on the West Coast.

Catherine, since the early days, has expanded her resume to include work in films and television series with many of the top well-known Actors and actresses. Dame Maggie Smith, Ellen Burstyn, Sandra Bullock, Colin Firth, and even Burt Reynolds are among the list. This book is a testament to her never-ending perseverance and dedication not only to live out her dreams in the entertainment industries but to help others do the same.

—Lance Britt

LANCE BRITT BIOGRAPHY

Lance Britt founded *Across the Canvas Productions* in January of 1978. His mission is to give others the opportunities he was blessed with while growing up in the entertainment industry.

Since its inception, the company has produced projects in various mediums, such as music, series for television, works of art, short films, features, and published works.

Lance, through his work with others on six continents and some islands in between, spreads love around the world one note at a time. He supports causes, charities, and worthwhile endeavors every moment of every day throughout the year.

Across the Canvas Productions is an outlet for people aspiring to be a part of the entertainment industry.

Across the Canvas Productions is a global PR (Public Relations) company working with top industry professionals to help them gain more attention on the global market.

Across the Canvas Productions is a place where top industry professionals can give back to the entertainment industry.

CATHERINE SEWELL

Where raw talent meets real technique—your breakthrough is now.

TRADE SECRETS

Foreword(s) from Johnny Whitaker, Lance Britt, and JD Demers.

"REAL-TIME ROADMAP TO ACTING

"Before the curtain rises, know exactly how to shine straight from a seasoned actor who's walked the path."

A practical, experience-driven guide that equips actors with real-world tools, mindset mastery, and industry insight to build confidence, sharpen craft, and navigate acting with clarity.

"None of us will ever accomplish anything excellent or commanding except when he listens to this whisper which is heard by him alone."
Trade Secrets
Releasing 2026
www.donnaink.shop
www.donnaink.net

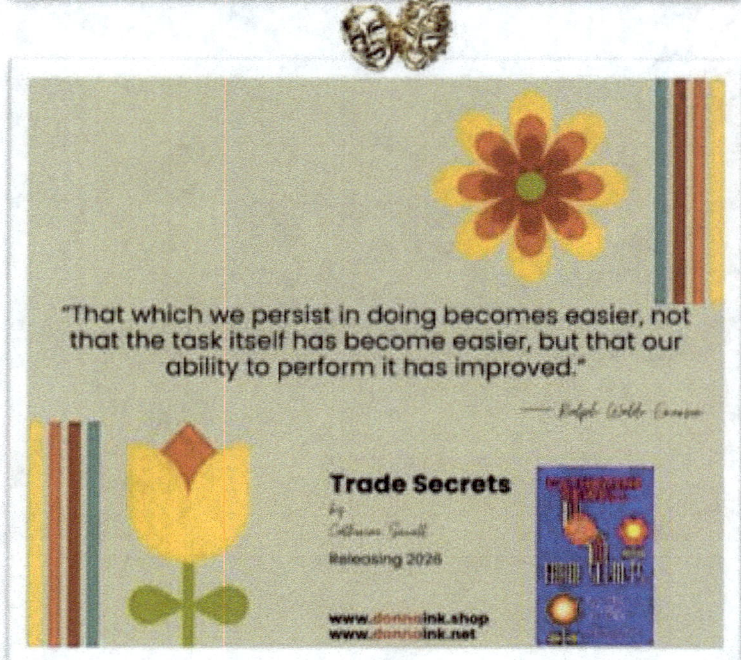
"That which we persist in doing becomes easier, not that the task itself has become easier, but that our ability to perform it has improved."
Trade Secrets
Releasing 2026
www.donnaink.shop
www.donnaink.net

FOREWORD THREE

JD DEMERS

JD DEMERS
Credit: IMDb

JD DEMERS
Credit: IMDb

There is a quiet majesty in the craft of acting — a discipline where vulnerability becomes strength, and the most honest work often rises from the silence between the lines. For those of us fortunate enough to live inside this world — not only as performers and creators, but as members of the *Screen Actors Guild (SAG)* — we understand that art means nothing without the work behind it. The courage. The repetition. The refinement.

It is in this sacred space that Catherine Sewell has long stood — steady, luminous, and wholly committed to the truth of the craft.

TRADE SECRETS: Real-Time Roadmap to Acting is more than a book; it is a masterclass shaped by lived experience. Catherine has poured into these pages the distilled wisdom of decades spent in front of the camera and in the quiet discipline of preparation. What she offers is not a formula. It is a generous, hard-won gift to Actors navigating an industry that is both deeply rewarding and often opaque.

I have had the privilege of serving as Catherine's Agent, publicist, and friend. And I can say with certainty: *what she brings to the set is matched only by what she brings to the people around her*. Her professionalism is unwavering. Her instincts are sharp. Her devotion to her peers and to the integrity of the work is rare. Alongside her husband and creative partner, Danny Sewell, she has built a life grounded in artistry and authenticity — proof that when the personal and professional are aligned, *excellence* becomes a natural byproduct.

This book pulses with real-time insight — the kind you cannot learn from theory alone. These lessons come from auditions, call-backs, set calls, table reads, script breakdowns, and the countless unseen hours where Actors shape themselves into storytellers. Catherine writes the way she acts *with nuance, generosity, and unmistakable fire*. She reminds us that talent is a muscle, not a miracle; that acting is work, not whimsy; and that success is built not only on what you know, but on how deeply you believe in the story you are telling.

To every actor stepping onto a stage or into a frame, searching for direction in the fog — let *Trade Secrets* be your compass. Catherine's voice is not only instructive; it is encouraging, steady, and deeply rooted in truth.

And trust me: there is no better guide for your artistic journey!

—JD Demers

JD DEMERS BIOGRAPHY

JD Demers (sometimes credited as Jonathon Demers, John Demers) is an American actor, producer, and creative professional with a diverse career spanning film, television, stage, and behind-the-scenes work. As a multi-faceted actor and producer, JD's career spans over two decades. He has appeared in independent films, historical dramas, and television series, while also contributing behind the scenes as a producer and technical advisor. His recent projects (*Clocked Out*, *Sans Toi*, and *Revelator*) show his continued commitment to diverse storytelling.

Career beginnings: Demers began appearing in independent films and shorts in the early 2000s, quickly establishing himself as a versatile performer capable of playing both dramatic and comedic roles.

Range of credits: His work includes acting, producing, writing, and technical advising. He has appeared in historical dramas, thrillers, family films, and faith-based projects.

Notable collaborations: He has worked alongside well-known Actors such as Eric Roberts (*Unbridled*) and appeared in productions tied to Warner Bros. (*Gods and Generals*).

Versatility: Demers has played judges, detectives, neighbors, and historical figures. He is also credited with voice work, hosting, and commercial acting.

Behind the camera: In addition to acting, Demers has served as producer, casting Director, Assistant Director, and Health Safety Supervisor on various projects.

Recent work: He continues to act in independent films and streaming projects, with credits in *Clocked-Out* (2024), *Sans Toi* (2025), and *Revelator* (upcoming).

YEAR	TITLE	ROLE
2000	*The Bone Yard* (TV Movie)	Producer credit
2002	*The Big White Wall*	Associate Producer
2004	*Massacre at Shelton Laurel*	Attorney Jonathan Sharpe (also Producer)
2008	*Will to Power*	Producer
2010	*The Rusty Bucket Kids: Lincoln, Journey to 16*	Aesop Traveler 1 (as Jonathon Demers)
2013	*Remnants*	Role (as Jonathon Demers)
2014	*Split Second*	Bags

YEAR	TITLE	ROLE
2014	*Vandroid (Music Video)*	Dick Daniels
2015	*Ghostlight*	Mr. Wellman
2017	*Unbridled*	Jim Martin (also Producer)
2017	*The Believers*	Espo
2018	*American Animals*	Used Car Salesman (uncredited)
2018	*Work Force*	Private Eye
2021	*Ninety Sunsets*	Henry Miller
2023	*Lemonopoly*	Doug Whitman
2024	*Clocked-Out (Short)*	Robert
2025	*Sans Toi (Short)*	Robert
Upcoming	*Revelator*	Detective Hoyt

TELEVISION

YEAR	TITLE	ROLE
1999–2012	*UNC-TV PBS Festival*	Host
2000s	*The Prosecutors* (multiple episodes)	Prosecutor Hart / Dr. Withers / Prosecutor James
2000s	*Flight from Justice*	Agent Thompson
2000s	*Gods and Generals*	Maj. Gen. Richard Ewell
2016	*Homicide Hunter*	Principal Tim Lewis
2018	*The FW!* (Miniseries)	Captain Bob Wilson

YEAR	TITLE	ROLE
2024	*History's Heroes: The Rusty Bucket Kids*	Shadow Man (pre-production)

OTHER WORKS

- **Producer credits:** *Unbridled* (2017), *Will to Power* (2008), and *The Rusty Bucket Kids* (2010).
- **Technical advisor:** *Among Brothers* (2005).
- **Health safety supervisor:** *No Vacancy* (2022), *Condor's Nest* (2023).

CREDIT

- Actors Access Resume
- Backstage Profile
- IMDb

"In all labor there is profit,
but idle chatter leads only to poverty."
Trade Secrets
Releasing 2026
www.donnaink.shop
www.donnaink.net

"Repetition helps learning."
Trade Secrets
Releasing 2026
www.donnaink.shop
www.donnaink.net

PREFACE

REASONS BEHIND THE QUILL

BEHIND THE CURTAIN: REFLECTIONS FROM MY PATH

W*hy did I embark on this literary journey?*

Let me share the secrets inked in this twenty-six-year odyssey.

The Chronicles Of A Twenty-Six-Year Odyssey

I craved a detailed, organized account—a chronicle of my life's work and experiences spanning two decades. The stage, the screen, the auditions—I wanted to capture it all. You see, memory is a fickle companion. Without written records, the details fade like footprints in the sand..

A Gift For Generations

This book isn't just for me; it's a legacy for our children, grandchildren, and kindred spirits. A glimpse into the whirlwind of opportunities, struggles, and triumphs that shaped my path. As the curtain rises on each chapter, they'll witness my life unfold—a tapestry woven with sweat, tears, and applause.

A BEACON FOR ASPIRING ACTORS

But there's more. As I dipped my quill, a revelation dawned. *Why not share these TRADE SECRETS as a beacon for aspiring actors?* Each page becomes a teaching experience for those

hungry for a career in the business. After all, I was once a teacher and life events are ripe for transformation into 'teachable moments'.

AN INVITATION BACKSTAGE

So, dear reader, join me backstage. The spotlight awaits, and the script unfolds. Let's explore the journey—the highs, the lows, and the whispered secrets that echo through the hallowed halls of entertainment.

The stage is set. **Let the curtain rise!**

PRELIMINARY QUESTIONS AND CONSIDERATIONS

Use the following section to establish a baseline of self understanding regarding the pursuit of acting, film, theater, voiceovers, and more. These questions are additionally included in the workbook Extro at the back of this book. Answering these questions now and then again later may demonstrate just how much growth and adaptation you will experience on your journey into the arts!

Initial Considerations

1. Are you interested in acting as a profession, a topic of research, or as a part-time resource or hobby?

____

____

____

____

2. Have you considered the time investment, research and / or training that will be needed based on your above choice or choices?

____

____

____

____

3. In considering a career or part-time hobby in acting, what is your focus on?

____

____

4. Do you foresee yourself being seen on the big screen or on the stage?

5. How much time are you willing to dedicate to consider it as a career versus a hobby?

6. Do you know anything about acting?

7. Is acquiring training a necessary consideration?

8. What are the basics you need to know about acting?

9. Are you more interested in drama or comedy?

10. Based on your choice of drama or comedy, your training may diverge slightly based on this decision.

11. Is acquiring training a necessary consideration?

12. What are the basics you need to know about acting?

13. Are you more interested in drama or comedy?

14. Based on your choice of drama or comedy, your training may diverge some based on your decision.

15. How do you believe you want to approach learning to act?

16. Do you want to research online about acting?

17. Do you want to take classes with acting instructors in person or online classes?

___

___

___

___

18. Do you want to begin by reading a book written by a trained and experienced actor?

___

___

___

___

"We all have our own life to pursue, our own kind of Dream to be weaving. And we all have some power to make wishes come true, as long as we keep believing."
—Louisa May Alcott
Trade Secrets
by
Catherine Sewell
Releasing 2026
www.donnaink.shop
www.donnaink.net

"Acknowledgment is not only gratitude — it is a foundation for growth. By honoring those who guide you, you strengthen your craft and your community."
—Catherine Sewell
Trade Secrets
by
Catherine Sewell
Releasing 2026
www.donnaink.shop
www.donnaink.net

ACKNOWLEDGMENTS

CATHERINE SEWELL

Thanks to the love of my life, my husband Danny L. Sewell, for being there and supporting me every step of the way in this challenging business and in writing this book. Danny has made my journey much more fun and exciting just by being by my side.

Many thanks to our children and grandchildren. Special thanks to my cousin by marriage, Mary Ayers, for traveling with me, supporting me, and being interested in my career.

I owe much gratitude and appreciation to Betty Caldwell for all her hard work doing the initial editing of my book. She spent many hours reading and editing, and I appreciate her generosity with her time and effort to help me. Many thanks I give to Lance Britt, founder and producer of *Across the Canvas Productions*, for editing and formatting my pictures and for the cover photo. Another friend,

Leah E. Perry has also spent endless hours helping me finalize my book.

To my agents who have had faith in me and helped me progress in my career, starting with Sherman Carmichael (one of my first agents), Phil Newsome of *Actors and Entertainment*, Anne and Rudy Greene of *Talent One*, Sylvia Hutson and staff of *Hutson Talent Agency*, Dawn and George Landrum and family of *Landrum Arts LA.*, and Renee Vesci and Genna Long-Bonner of *Fast Lane Talent Agency*. Renee Vesci started this journey with me dating back to my early years in the business. We were in several films together, and currently, she is my North Carolina agent along with her partner Genna Long-Bonner. The Landrum family has been my agents since 2007 and have supported and worked hard for me all these years. Through hard work, dedication, and ethical behavior they are rated among the top agencies in the country. The support and guidance from all the above agents have been invaluable to me as I develop and grow in my craft.

I also wish to express sincere thanks to Johnny Whitaker, JD Demers, and Lance Britt for contributing their thoughtful Forewords to this title. Your words set the stage with insight and encouragement, and I am honored to have your voices opening this work. To all who have supported me, mentored me, and believed in me, your influence has shaped my craft and my career.

INTRODUCTION

TRADE SECRETS
A JOURNEY THROUGH THE FOOTLIGHTS

Welcome to the dazzling **World Of Entertainment**! *TRADE SECRETS* is more than a mere memoir; it is your backstage pass to the highs, lows, and limelight of a career spanning from 1997 to 2024 (and perhaps beyond). Buckle up as we traverse the glittering stages, the silver screens, and the hallowed halls of creativity.

ACT I: THE GENRE TAPESTRY

UNVEILING THE CANVAS

You've worked in many corners of this business. You've spent time in film, television, commercials, corporate pieces, and theatre. You've also done voiceover and music. Every one of those paths has taught you something useful and helped shape the artist you are today..

THE ART OF MASTERY

Working in this field means learning a lot of different skills. You've taken on many roles and learned how to adjust to whatever the job needed. Being good at several things is not easy. It takes steady work, real training, and a willingness to keep improving. You've focused on building your acting skills with care. Each area of the industry has its own way of doing

things, and its own expectations. The tools of the trade, computers, cameras, audio equipment, and lighting, are part of what helps you do the job well.

ACT II: THE SPECIAL INTERLUDES

BEHIND THE VELVET CURTAIN

Between the main parts of your story, we take time to look at the work behind the scenes. This is where we talk about the business itself, the auditions, the callbacks, and the moments that move your career forward. We look at the skills that matter, like building chemistry on camera, understanding stage movement, and shaping a character from the inside out. These sections are meant to guide you, the same way a good mentor would, offering steady advice from the background..

THE GOLDEN NUGGETS

At the end of each chapter, you will find a few helpful takeaways. They aren't just lists of what to do or avoid. They're small pieces of guidance meant to help you move forward in this business. Whether you're preparing for an audition or learning how to handle the day-to-day challenges of the industry, these notes are here to point you in the right direction.

ACT III: THE EVOLUTION

HOW THE INDUSTRY HAS CHANGED

Over the years, this industry has shifted in big ways. Film moved from physical reels to digital work, and the tools we use have changed right along with it. Even though the technology looks different now, your growth has come from the same steady things it always has. Training, consistency, and learning how to work well with agents have all shaped the path you are on.

LOOKING AHEAD

There is more to come. Your work does not end at the twenty-year mark. Your experience will keep growing and new opportunities will meet you as you continue to show up and do the work. What matters most is not how many projects you take on, but the quality of the work you bring to each one. Your next chapter is waiting, and the lessons in Trade Secrets will continue to guide you.

Trade Secrets is more than a book. It reflects the life of a performer, the work behind the scenes, and the heart you bring to your craft.

So, step into Trade Secrets.

Your cue is here.

Various Acting Considerations

This is not an exhaustive list. Most talents can be utilized in the entertainment business. The following categories highlight the wide range of acting opportunities available, followed skill set lists that often support or enhance an actor's career. Many performers discover that their unique combination of abilities opens unexpected doors; sometimes, the skills you least expect become the ones that book the job.

1. Acting Categories

These are the primary performance avenues where actors may work, train, or specialize:

2. On-Camera Acting

☐ Commercials (National / Regional / Local)
☐ Documentary Reenactments
☐ Film (Feature / Short)
☐ Independent Films
☐ Industrials / Corporate Videos
☐ Music Videos
☐ Reality TV (Host / Participant / Reenactment)
☐ Student Films
☐ Television (Network / Cable / Streaming)
☐ Web Series / Digital Content

3. Live & Stage Performance

☐ Cruise Ship Entertainment
☐ Dinner Theatre

☐ Immersive / Interactive Theatre
☐ Live Event Hosting / Emceeing
☐ Theatre (Musical / Non-Musical)
☐ Theme Park Shows
☐ Touring Theatre

4. **Specialized Acting Work**
☐ Body Double
☐ Extras / Background
☐ Green Screen / Virtual Production Acting
☐ Improvisation
☐ Motion Capture (MoCap)
☐ Performance Capture
☐ Photo Double
☐ Sketch Comedy
☐ Stand-In
☐ Stand-Up Comedy

5. **Voice & Audio Performance**
☐ ADR (Automated Dialogue Replacement)
☐ Audiobook Narration
☐ Podcast Performance
☐ Radio Drama
☐ Voiceover (Commercial / Animation / Promo)

6. **Hosting & Presenting**
☐ Corporate Presenter
☐ Interviewer / Reporter
☐ Red Carpet Host
☐ Spokesperson
☐ TV Host

ASSOCIATED ARTS & SKILL SETS

These are the abilities, disciplines, and special skills that enhance an actor's versatility and marketability. Many are highly sought after in casting.

1. **Vocal & Audio Skills**
    - ☐ Audio Prompter / Ear-Prompter
    - ☐ Dialects / Accents
    - ☐ Fluent Languages
    - ☐ Narration Skills
    - ☐ Singing / Vocal Range
    - ☐ Voiceover Technique
2. **Movement & Physical Performance**
    - ☐ Circus Arts (Aerial / Silks / Trapeze)
    - ☐ Clowning
    - ☐ Dance (Any Style)
    - ☐ Falls / Fight Choreography
    - ☐ Horseback Riding
    - ☐ Ice Skating
    - ☐ Juggling
    - ☐ Martial Arts
    - ☐ Motorcycling
    - ☐ Precision Driving
    - ☐ Puppetry
    - ☐ Roller Skating / Rollerblading
    - ☐ Stage Combat
    - ☐ Stunts
    - ☐ Swimming / Diving
    - ☐ Weaponry (Swords / Firearms / Archery)
    - ☐ Yoga / Pilates / Flexibility
3. **Musical & Artistic Skills**
    - ☐ Beatboxing / Vocal Percussion
    - ☐ DJ / Mixing
    - ☐ Musical Instruments
    - ☐ Singing (Classical / Contemporary / Theatre)
    - ☐ Songwriting
    - ☐ Visual Arts (Painting / Drawing)
4. **Technical & Production Skills**
    - ☐ Audio Recording

- ☐ Camera Operation
- ☐ Green Screen Awareness
- ☐ Lighting Basics
- ☐ Motion Capture Suit Work
- ☐ Teleprompter Operation
- ☐ Video or Audio Editing

5. **Professional & Practical Skills**
   - ☐ Bartending / Barista Skills
   - ☐ Carpentry / Set Construction
   - ☐ Childcare Experience
   - ☐ Culinary Skills / Chef
   - ☐ Driving Stick Shift
   - ☐ Good with Pets / Animal Handling
   - ☐ Journalism / Reporter Experience
   - ☐ Law Enforcement Experience
   - ☐ Medical Training (CPR / EMT / Nursing)
   - ☐ Military Experience
   - ☐ Public Speaking
   - ☐ Sewing / Costume Repair
   - ☐ Sign Language (ASL or other)
   - ☐ Strong Cold-Read Skills
   - ☐ Teaching / Coaching
   - ☐ Unusual Special Skills (Fire Eating, Escape Artistry, etc.)

TOP FIVE SKILLS TO DEVELOP

Use this page to identify the five skills that will most strengthen your craft, expand your opportunities, or elevate your marketability. Choose from the Acting Categories, Skill Set Lists, or add your own.

SKILLS I INTEND TO DEVELOP

1	
2	

3	
4	
5	

INTRODUCING THE WORKBOOK

In the back matter of *TRADE SECRETS,* you will find *The Development Workbook,* this is a personal studio space de-signed for deeper reflection, intentional planning, consistent practice, and meaningful growth. Inside are guided prompts, real-world exercises, tracking pages for auditions and training, and tools to help you strengthen both your professional presence and your artistic identity. This is where your story begins to take shape, where inspiration and knowledge turn into action and momentum.

Whether you're stepping into the industry for the first time or refining your craft after years of experience, *TRADE SECRETS* becomes a practical, personal extension of my journey — and the one you're stepping into next.

Your cue awaits; let's begin.

"Every artist was first an amateur."
Trade Secrets
Releasing 2026
www.donnaink.shop
www.donnaink.net

"He has not learned the lesson of life who does not every day surmount a fear."
Trade Secrets
Releasing 2026
www.donnaink.shop
www.donnaink.net

HOW TO USE THE BOOK

THE STRUCTURE

Each chapter of *TRADE SECRETS* follows a consistent design so you can move through it with ease:

- **Chapter and Sub-chapter Titles** — establish the theme and focus and deliver my story.
- **Behind the Curtain: Reflections from My Path** — personal stories that illustrate the theme and invite you to connect.
- **Quotes** — highlighted insights, often more than one, to pause and reflect on featured throughout this title.
- **Reader Prompts** — questions designed to help you explore your own journey.
- **Actor Development Guide Integration** — structured exercises including mentor acknowledgments, motivator identification, reflection guide, questionnaire, and a closing thought.

YOUR INVITATION

This book is designed not only to be read but to be experienced. The reflections are here to spark resonance, the quotes to inspire, and the prompts to encourage you to pause and write. The workbook pages are rehearsal space for your growth

— places where you can practice, explore, and return again and again.

HOW TO ENGAGE

- Read the stories that open doors.
- Pause for quotes and prompts — let them stir up your own thoughts.
- Write in the margins, answer the questions, and treat the exercises as practice for your own stage.
- Revisit often; your answers will evolve as you do.

A Living Journey

This is not a book to rush through. It is meant to be lived in. The structure will guide you, but the spotlight belongs to you.

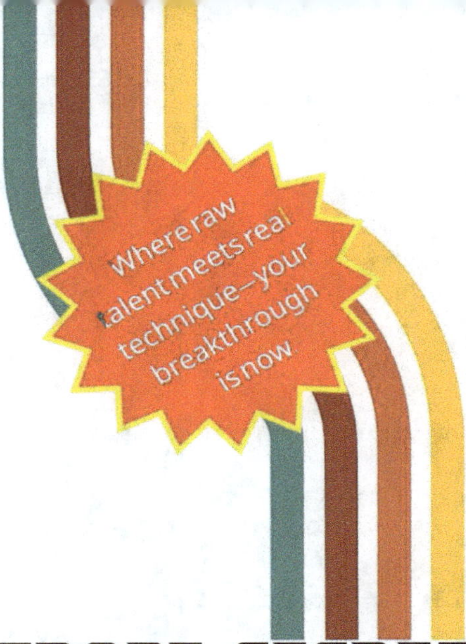
Where raw
talent meets real
technique—your
breakthrough
is now

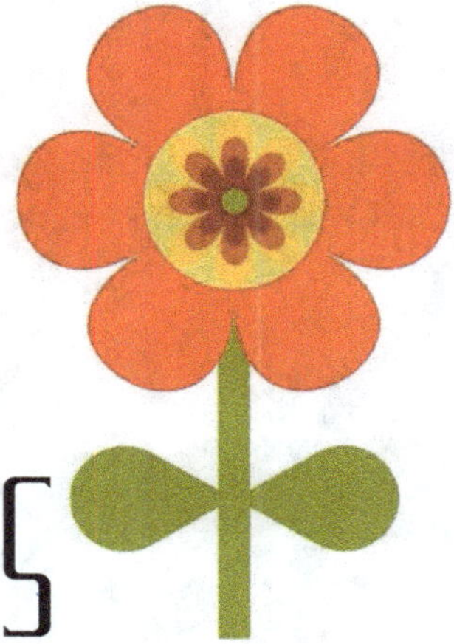

TRADE SECRETS

CATHERINE SEWELL

Forward(s) by Johnny Whitaker,
Lance Britt, and JD Demers.

REAL-TIME ROADMAP TO ACTING

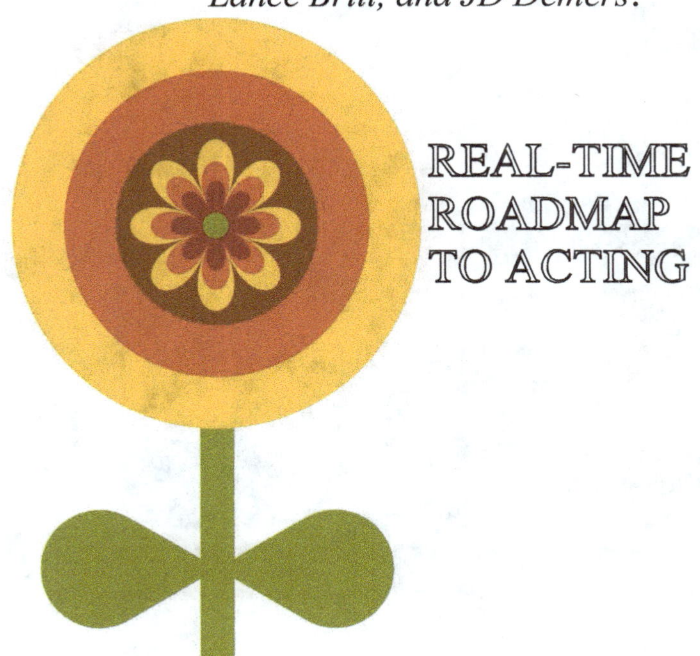

"Actors and audience share a unique bond—the magic of a moment that can never be repeated."
Trade Secrets
Releasing 2026
www.donnaink.shop
www.donnaink.net

"Our truest response to the irrationality of the world is to paint or sing or write, for only in such response do we find truth."
Trade Secrets
Releasing 2026
www.donnaink.shop
www.donnaink.net

CHAPTER ONE

CAREER CHANGE...HOW IT STARTED

BEHIND THE CURTAIN: REFLECTIONS FROM MY PATH

Once upon a time, in the heart of the middle age, life began to play its peculiar tricks. *The world around me seemed to shift, or was it I who yearned for a change? Was it the infamous midlife crisis knocking at my door, or a simple refusal to 'settle'? Should I settle for monotony, for unfulfillment, for stagnation, and a myriad of other unsatisfactory states?*

In the grand scheme of life, we often spend the first half preparing for a career that promises success, a career that can support our chosen lifestyle. We pour our time and effort into this pursuit. In my case, this meant a journey through four years of college and graduate school. After many years of dedication, I finally held a doctorate degree in my hands.

I had specialized in counseling, psychology, and school administration, believing that this would be my life's work, my source of joy. I was convinced that a good education and a fulfilling job would bring me the best things in life.

However, when we choose our careers, our decisions are not always guided by our true desires. Sometimes, we are swayed by the 'hot' field of the moment, the promise of wealth, the expectations of our parents, the path of least resistance in school, and countless other factors. I chose to become a teacher during an era when women were predominantly teachers, nur-

ses, or secretaries. My family tree was filled with educators—my mother, my sister, aunts, uncles, and other relatives.

As a teacher, I had my share of memorable moments. There were days filled with laughter, days filled with learning, and days filled with the pure joy of seeing a student's eyes light up with understanding. But as time passed, I began to realize that while teaching was a noble profession, it might not be my final destination.

And so, my journey continues, ever in search of that elusive 'something more'. Because, after all, who says middle age is the end of the road? Perhaps, it's just the beginning of a new adventure.

Once upon a time, at the tender age of twenty-one, I embarked on a journey as a teacher. I found myself teaching various grades across different school systems in two states, all while my husband served his four-year military tour. But as the years passed, a nagging feeling of discontent began to grow within me. Teaching, a profession that had been a perfect fit for my relatives, somehow didn't seem to suit me. Despite my love for the children and the rewarding experience of teaching them, it lacked the spark that I yearned for.

Every morning, I woke up longing for a career that would ignite my passion. That's when it struck me - I could pivot within the realm of education. My first step was to explore other areas that might pique my interest. This led me to a four-year stint as a guidance counselor. It was more fulfilling, and I loved working with the students, but I still craved something that would satisfy my creative desires.

The school system, facing a shortage of school psychologists, proposed that I return to school for further training. The idea was appealing, and I was convinced that this career choice would finally ignite my passion. So, armed with more graduate work beyond my master's degree, I joined the ranks as an official school psychologist.

A few years later, I was promoted to a central office administrative position. This role was exciting and allowed me to tap into the 'right side of my brain' - the side that fuels our creativity and imagination. However, due to political circumstances, my position changed, and I found myself back in graduate school, this time pursuing a doctorate in administration.

With my newly minted doctorate degree, I set out with high hopes of career happiness. But the search for the right administrative position proved to be a futile endeavor. It was a time when upper-level administrative positions were being cut rather than added. To survive and afford life's niceties, I returned to the one career where I could always find a position - school psychology.

I worked in this field for another four years, but eventually, the constant testing and psychological evaluations took their toll. Testing became the main priority, leaving little time to offer a continuum of services to the students. And so, my journey continues, ever in search of that elusive 'something more'.

In the aftermath of a burnout, I found myself at a crossroads. As an educator, I was left pondering my next move. The idea of becoming a university instructor seemed enticing - a role that promised prestige and excitement, albeit with a modest salary.

However, as I embarked on this new journey, I soon realized I was still wandering down the wrong path. During my tenure at the university, an opportunity arose for a psychologist in the same county where I was teaching. The offer was tempting - good pay for part-time work. So, I decided to give it another shot, only to find myself returning to the familiar and secure. I was caught in a cycle, circling the same path, far from *The Road Less Traveled. Where was the joy, the passion?* I was merely surviving, securing my existence, much like everyone else. The passion for a career I loved remained elusive. But sometimes, life has a way of throwing curve-balls to steer us in a new direction. And that's precisely what happened to me.

I once read that to find our true passion, we should look back to when we were twelve years old. The interests we had at that age are often the ones we would truly enjoy in our adult lives. At that age, we are free to explore and discover what we love, unburdened by the responsibilities of work and maintaining a household. But who has the time to reminisce about childhood when you're busy raising a family and working in a career you've spent your life training for?

As a young child in grammar school, I loved to sing. I would enter talent contests with a friend, and we would delight in choosing the song, deciding on our outfits, and choreographing our dance routine. I also sang in the school and church choirs. Unfortunately, my school didn't offer drama, and my town lacked a local theater.

Looking back, I realize that these were the moments when I felt truly alive. These were the moments that sparked joy and passion. And perhaps, these are the moments that will guide me towards a career that I can truly love.

During my college years, I had the opportunity to dip my toes into the world of acting. Despite my lack of experience, I was cast in a play. I was in the running for the lead role but ended up as the understudy. Looking back, I realize that my heavy Southern accent may have played a part in that decision. The lead role went to a woman without a Southern accent, from another state. Interestingly, my instructor was also from a different state (Northern). But more on this accent business later, so stay tuned!

Back then, and even now to a large extent, we are conditioned to make career decisions based on practical and realistic expectations. Pursuing a career in drama or voice in the South during the 1970s or 1980s would have likely led to standing in the unemployment line. Dreaming big and pursuing it against all odds wasn't as popular as it is now, especially in show business. Unless one could move to California or New York, achieving that dream would have been extremely challenging.

In the final years of my tenure with the school system, I got a taste of Hollywood. Quite by accident, I learned about a talent agent who helped aspiring individuals kick-start their careers in the entertainment industry. During a conversation with a photographer, I expressed my desire for a change from the field of education. She introduced me to her sister, a talent agent, who subsequently accepted me into her agency in North Carolina.

I began my journey in the film industry as an 'Extra' or 'Background' worker. These are the individuals you see in the background of movies, playing non-speaking parts. After two years of getting a taste of the industry, I felt a fire within me, a desire for more. As my work in school psychology became increasingly demanding and detrimental to my health, I decided to take a break from education. It was time to pursue my dream.

I decided to rekindle the old passions of my youth and venture into the acting profession in my middle years. This marked the beginning of a new journey, one filled with excitement, adventure, fantasy, and fulfillment. But let me add, it also came with its fair share of frustration, rejection, humiliation, hard work, and long hours. But I want you to know if I can reach my dreams, so can you! Age should never be a barrier, as you will see with me.

AUTHOR'S NOTATIONS

Do not be afraid to take some risks in your life. I would suggest that they be 'planned' risks. In other words, start with a well-designed plan and consider any possible contingences so that you are better prepared.

Being able to financially support yourself while pursing your dream is a necessity unless you have other available funds. Actors usually try to find jobs that are flexible to allow time away. Part-time work may also be a good option. Retirees will often do extra / background work almost exclusively for fun with the added benefit of some pay.

ACTOR TRAINING INSIGHTS & TIDBITS

Key Points to Consider

- Actors who realize this is a business tend to be more successful.
- Being successful means learning about this business and having a reasonable perspective. Misconceptions and expectations can be discouraging.
- Learning something about the jobs others perform in this industry can be very helpful.
- Choose positive, disciplined and hardworking people to hang out with.

"Find a job you enjoy doing, and you will never have to work a day in your life."
Trade Secrets
Releasing 2026
www.donnaink.shop
www.donnaink.net

"When you have exhausted all possibilities, remember this - you haven't."
—Thomas Edison
Trade Secrets
by
Catherine Sewell
Releasing 2026
www.donnaink.shop
www.donnaink.net

CHAPTER TWO

THE BEGINNING, 1997

Once upon a time, on a day I remember vividly, I received a call from my Agent. I had been selected as an extra for TNT's *The Day Lincoln Was Shot,* a *TV Movie of the Week* (MOW). The anticipation had been building for this day, and finally, it arrived - July 7, 1997.

A group of us, all budding Actors, gathered in Durham. We boarded a chartered bus that would take us to our destination - an old theater nestled in the heart of downtown Richmond, Virginia. The air was thick with excitement as we journeyed towards our first taste of the limelight.

Upon arrival, we checked in, completed our pay vouchers, and we were ushered into hair and makeup. This was a new experience for me, one that was both thrilling and nerve-wracking. We were dressed in period clothing, the women in long, full dresses complete with hooped petticoats. The men donned Civil War uniforms, which proved to be quite warm for a July day.

Our hair was styled to match the era. Mine was parted down the middle, flat on top, with the rest pulled back and adorned with a curly hairpiece. To add to the authenticity, they removed all my carefully applied lipstick and replaced it with powder. We were sternly warned against applying any lipstick. One girl was even accused of doing so, but she politely explained her lips were naturally that color.

After hours of preparation, we were finally ready. We crossed the street to the theater, our stage for the day. Being near

the back of the line, I was seated in the balcony of the 'pretend' *Ford's Theater*. We spent the day oscillating between the theater and the 'holding area,' where extras wait until they are called on set. Often, we spent more time 'holding' than on the set.

Despite the long hours and the waiting, a spark of excitement ignited within me. This was just the beginning of my journey into the world of acting, a journey that would lead me to discover my true passion.

No movie would be complete without its stars. Lance Henriksen, best known as the android 'Bishop' in *Aliens* and his starring role in the TV series *Millennium*, played Lincoln. Mrs. Lincoln was portrayed by Donna Murphy, a renowned figure in musical theater and television. Rob Morrow of *Northern Exposure* fame was another main star. Fr0m a distance, they looked just as they did on television. I had the opportunity to speak to Donna Murphy and shake her hand. She was a vision of beauty, especially in her stunning gown. Meeting the stars and hearing snippets of information about them was always a thrill.

At the end of a long day and night of shooting, we were all ready to retreat to our beds. However, it was late into the night when the bus finally rolled into the parking lot in Durham. I still had an hour's ride home. The things we endure for a taste of fun and excitement!

When the movie aired on television in the fall, I was merely a black silhouette in the balcony. Only I, and the union soldier I walked in with could recognize who I was. It was a disappointment after telling all my family to look for me. I learned a valuable lesson that day - as an extra, do not tell people to look for you because most times you are not seen, or they cut you out. But that is alright. I had a great time, gained a wonderful experience, and earned a little money.

Most film extra work pays from $50.00 to $100.00 for eight-plus hours. You can earn overtime, but mostly on Union films. On independent films, the pay can be even lower.

Since making my television debut, I decided it was time to work on my Southern accent. If I was to be an actress, I needed to learn to speak the Standard English of news anchors and other movie stars. And so, my journey continues, ever in pursuit of my dream.

The next chapter of my journey was a daunting one. *How could I find someone who could help me shed my deeply ingrained Marlboro County, South Carolina accent?* This was no small task, because I had been speaking this way since my earliest memories. The lessons were challenging and felt foreign to me. Ironically, learning Spanish with an accent seemed easier.

I attended several lessons with a speech teacher, attempting to correct what I perceived as a problem. But then, the teacher moved, leaving me with the arduous task of finding a replacement. My search led me to be a private lesson teacher at a community college. However, she was only able to assist me with a few lessons. I could not help but think she found the task too daunting, too stressful.

With speech and diction classes on hold, I turned my attention to acting classes. I breathed a sigh of relief, thinking this wouldn't be as hard as changing my lifetime of speech habits. But even today, years later, I'm still grappling with Standard English.

But in the grand scheme of things, this struggle was just another stepping-stone on my journey. A journey filled with trials and triumphs, challenges and victories. And through it all, I have learned the road to success is not always smooth, but the journey is what makes the destination worthwhile.

AUTHOR'S NOTATIONS

One thing I learned right away is that you are kidding yourself if you think you can just 'sail to the top of the line'! In other words, anything worthwhile takes time and effort. Learn to temper your expectations so you will not be disappointed. Look for the lessons learned.

ACTOR TRAINING INSIGHTS & TIDBITS

Key Points to Consider

Patience is a virtue is a viable consideration as it is an admirable quality. Our instinct is to be impatient. All of us struggle with impatience; however, it is a skill that can be learned. Working in the film industry requires patience when waiting for your turn to go on set, in learning the craft of acting, and making advances in the industry. By learning patience and not setting our expectations too high, we don't become as frustrated and stressed.

- Know what the EXPECTATIONS are for every job you are asked for or required to do. Different kinds of acting may require a totally different skill base.
- Identifying your STRENGTHS and WEAKNESSES will help you to know what you need to spend time working and training on.
- Determine your TYPE (essentially your physicality; what you look, sound, and act or move like)
- Determine your BRAND (the image you want others to see when they think of you) your brand explains who you are. For example, authenticity.

Successful Actors work on their craft in some way every day. It may include something as varied as learning a new acting technique to learning a new accent. Start focusing on and developing the tools you will need for this business such as headshots, resume, and a reel.

The Day Lincoln Was Shot, a TV Movie of the Week.
It arrived - July 7, 1997.

"I hated every minute of training, but I said,
Don't quit. Suffer now and
live the rest of your life as a champion."
Trade Secrets
#eleasing 2026
www.donnaink.shop
www.donnaink.net

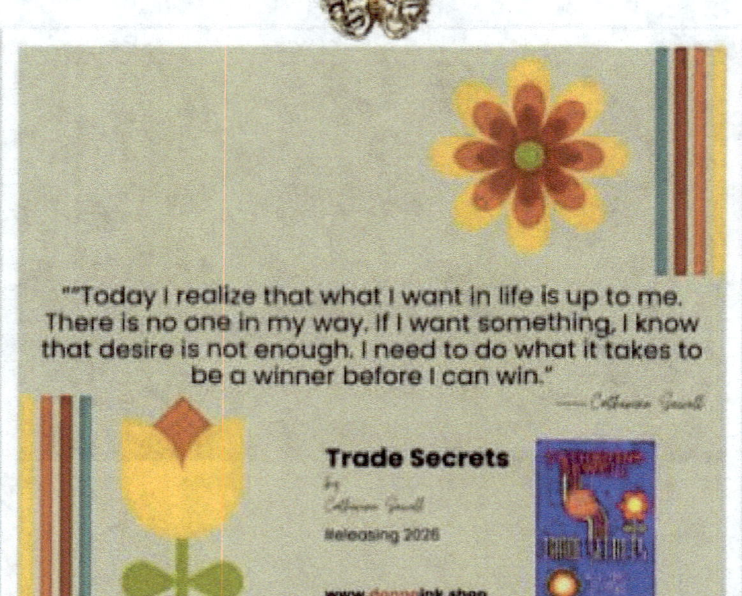
""Today I realize that what I want in life is up to me. There is no one in my way. If I want something, I know that desire is not enough. I need to do what it takes to be a winner before I can win."
Trade Secrets
#eleasing 2026
www.donnaink.shop
www.donnaink.net

CHAPTER THREE

THE CALL CAME...THE BIG SCREEN

As the sands of time slipped through the hourglass, it was January of 1998 when my Agent's call echoed through the silence. This was my second debut, but this time, it was for the big screen - *my first major motion picture*. The anticipation was palpable. Months had passed. I had begun to wonder if the call would ever come. I had auditioned for a local play and was on the verge of securing a part. But when the call for the movie came, I had to make a choice. I decided to drop out of the play. The allure of the big screen was too strong, especially with the tantalizing prospect of seeing Patrick Swayze in *Black Dog*.

The day of reckoning arrived. For two days, I was immersed in the world of movie-making in Charlotte, North Carolina. The first morning began before dawn. We convened at an old warehouse. After signing in and enduring a long wait, we were ferried by van to the sidewalks of downtown Charlotte. Our task was simple - to blend in as pedestrians. But as you can imagine, January day can be bitterly cold. We were asked not to wear coats as the movie was set in spring to summer. So, naturally, we were cold and had to keep moving to stay warm.

During the shooting, various bystanders would occasionally wander onto the location. One persistent woman was adamant about staying on the street where we were filming until she saw Patrick Swayze. Despite our assurances he was not even in Charlotte at the time, she remained undeterred. I certainly did not want to share my big chance of being seen on the big screen with her! Thankfully, she eventually gave up and left.

And so, my journey in the world of acting continued, filled with excitement, anticipation, and the occasional unexpected encounter.

At last, lunchtime arrived. We retreated to the warmth of the warehouse, eager to rest our weary feet and satiate our hunger. But in the world of movie-making, there is a pecking order. The Crew, Directors, Stars, and other important figures had to fill their plates first. This was a protocol that had to be followed, or one risked being reprimanded.

We approached the chuck wagon, a trailer where some of the food was cooked, and chose our meat. To my surprise, we were offered delicacies such as filet mignon and seafood. I had assumed such luxuries were reserved for the Stars and Directors. Once we had our meat, we helped ourselves to the vegetables, fruits, salads, and desserts spread out on long tables. It was a feast fitting for kings, and it helped to compensate for the modest day's pay.

By the time the day was over, exhaustion had set in. I could hardly move and wondered how I would muster the energy for the next day. Fortunately, the call time for the second day was not as early as the first. Knowing where to go, I did not have to rise as early to make the two-hour journey to Charlotte. In this business, your day may start early, especially if you have to travel an hour or more to the shoot. There were times when I found myself waking up as early as 2:30 to 3:00 am to travel.

And so, my journey in the world of acting continued, filled with early mornings, long days, and unforgettable experiences.

At the same warehouse location, an Assistant Director posed a question to us extras - *Would any of us like to drive our car for the next scene?* Before I could raise my hand, a woman, determined to be the first volunteer, nearly stampeded me in her haste. She knocked over a chair in the process; thankfully, it was not me she hit. After the commotion, the question was posed again. This time, I eagerly raised my hand and was se-lected. *What was I thinking?* I suppose I was driven by the desire to contribute and feel important.

And so, there I was, a woman who had just volunteered to drive her car on the freeway, despite not knowing the streets or highways of Charlotte at all. My sense of direction was so poor, I often joked I could hardly find my way out of a paper bag. When I received a map from a Production Assistant (PA), it might as well have been written in a foreign language. Map reading was Greek to me. When I asked him for more details about our route, his response was, "You are going to have to learn Charlotte."

Little did I know he was speaking the truth. Much of my work would be in Charlotte or the neighboring cities. My only option was to follow the rest of the drivers ahead of me and hope I did not lose sight of them. With a little prayer, we were off. I made sure to stay right behind the drivers ahead of me, even if it meant running at a red light. I was nervous about it because one of the very vocal Assistant Directors had warned us if we got caught for traffic violations, we would be 'off the movie.'

And so, my adventure in the world of acting continued, filled with unexpected challenges, thrilling opportunities, and memorable experiences.

Another strong direction that this Northern AD gave us was not to dare look at the helicopters that were filming while we were driving.

He practically threatened us with our lives if we looked at those helicopters. He told us with his heavy Northern accent, if we felt like we just had to look at those helicopters to go outside 'right now' and take a good look because when we started filming, we were not allowed the opportunity. So, after we were thoroughly intimidated and felt like kindergarteners, we went on our way to drive our cars on the predetermined path (without looking up at the helicopters).

Once upon a time, in the bustling world of film, I found myself immersed in an adventure that was as unpredictable as it was exciting. The highlight of each day was undoubtedly mealtime. *Ah, the joy of savoring fabulous meals! You can tell I'm a food enthusiast, can't you?*

On some sets, especially those teeming with extras, the culinary offerings were rather disappointing. A simple boxed lunch was the norm. However, when part of a small group of extras, the gastronomic experience can be quite delightful. Trust me, after a long day of shooting, food becomes a luxury. Lunchtime could be as late as 3:00 pm; usually six hours after the crew call time and then, your stomach is growling in anti-cipation.

One day, after a scene that required the use of my car, a thoughtful crew member filled up my gas tank. It was an unexpected gesture that added a touch of warmth to the cold winter days.

During my time on set, I was disappointed I didn't get to see Patrick Swayze or Randy Travis. They were not filming on the days I worked.

The long, grueling days, often stretching over 12 hours, coupled with the winter chill, made me question my decision to pursue this movie life. I realized the glamour of the film industry was just the tip of the iceberg.

When *Black Dog* was released, I eagerly watched, only to find my scene in Charlotte was a mere few seconds, and neither I nor my car was visible. I learned a valuable lesson - not to announce my participation until I saw the film myself.

Despite the initial disappointment, I chose to view it as a learning experience. I had fun, and more importantly, I had gained invaluable experience from a TV film and a feature film. Even though I was yet to be seen on screen, except as a black silhouette, I was ready for the next chapter of my journey in the enchanting world of film.

AUTHOR'S NOTATIONS

Oftentimes we tend to visualize and glamorize a new opportunity or job very differently than what the actual reality of the situation is. This can certainly be the case in 'show business.' The excitement of having that first experience can cloud our realistic expectations. This is why knowing what you may encounter beforehand by reading or training and being prepared makes for a better experience. There is nothing like experiencing every opportunity and making it your own!

Actor Training Insights & Tidbits

Key Points to Consider

Be informed and prepared before stepping into any new acting experience. Understand what the job requires and how you can show up prepared.

- Review any materials sent to you in advance so you know exactly what is expected.
- If you are doing extra or background work, read up and aim to be your best. (See the end of Chapter 9 for tips.)
- You do not need an Agent to secure extra/background roles. Many Facebook acting groups and online communities post opportunities regularly—some paid, some volunteer.
- Search casting sites in your state and join local acting groups to stay updated on new listings.
- Extra work is an excellent way to learn how the film and television industry operates. You can explore film sets, TV productions, or commercial shoots.

Chapter 9 includes additional survival tips for *Extras and Background Actors.*

"Every experience can be a potential life lesson."
—Catherine Sewell
Trade Secrets
by
Catherine Sewell
Releasing 2026
www.donnaink.shop
www.donnaink.net
CATHERINE SEWELL
TRADE SECRETS

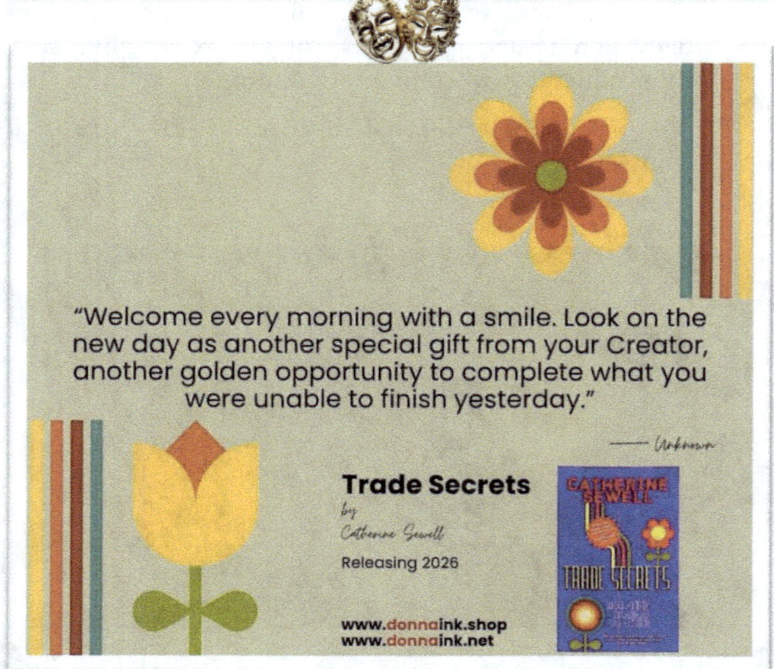
"Welcome every morning with a smile. Look on the new day as another special gift from your Creator, another golden opportunity to complete what you were unable to finish yesterday."
—Unknown
Trade Secrets
by
Catherine Sewell
Releasing 2026
www.donnaink.shop
www.donnaink.net
CATHERINE SEWELL
TRADE SECRETS

CHAPTER FOUR

CO-HOST OF LIVE AT NINE

In the wake of my latest cinematic endeavor, a period of respite unfolded before me, a chance to shake off the rigors of the silver screen. Yet, the allure of the lens was irresistible. A hiatus of five months loomed ahead, but the siren calls of the camera beckoned me to hone my craft.

With a blend of trepidation and excitement, I found myself at the doorstep of our local broadcasting beacon, *WBF-TV Channel 46*. A dialogue with the station's general manager sparked an opportunity to dip my toes into the world of live television. Woody Seymour, the charismatic host of *Live at Nine*, was my point of contact.

Woody, foreseeing a challenging interview with an upcoming guest, welcomed the idea of an additional presence on the show. His faith in my potential was both daunting and invigorating. The prospect of co-hosting was a leap from my comfort zone, a far cry from the days when the mere thought of speaking on camera or radio would send tremors down my spine.

The day of my television debut arrived. A wave of apprehension washed over me, compelling me to consider an escape route. I reached out to Woody, citing a sudden bout of back troubles as my excuse. But Woody, a fellow sufferer of back issues, was unyielding. His encouragement was the nudge I needed to face my fears.

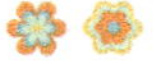

So, I took the plunge. My first appearance was a study in nerves, my demeanor akin to a statue, my voice emerging only when absolutely necessary. Woody's introductions were my lifeline until I found my own voice. This was the start of my journey, a step towards mastering the art of live television, a testament to the power of stepping out of one's comfort zone.

As if in the blink of an eye, a decade plus one had danced by since my inaugural night on *Live at Nine*. The journey to confidence, to feeling at home under the unblinking gaze of the camera, was a marathon, not a sprint. Yet, by the time I bid adieu to the show, my notes and scripted questions had be-come mere relics of the past. This transformation stands as a testament to the power of perseverance, a beacon for those grappling with the fear of public speaking.

Our shows were a delightful medley of meticulous planning and spontaneous hilarity. The unpredictability of live television often caught us off guard, catapulting us back on air before we could catch our breath. Yet, every stumble, every on-air jest was met with laughter, both from us and our audience. These unscripted moments, these instances of genuine human connection, were the heart of our show.

Whether we were broadcasting from the bustling local fair, the familiar confines of our studio, or other vibrant locations, each show was a live wire, a thrilling exercise in adaptability. This journey introduced me to a kaleidoscope of fascinating individuals and deepened my understanding of our community.

As an educator at heart, I saw each episode as an opportunity for learning, a chance to leave our viewers a little wiser, a little more informed. Each show culminated with me sharing a favorite quotation, nuggets of wisdom that had fueled my own journey. These words of encouragement, these pearls of wisdom, can be a beacon for anyone venturing into the entertainment industry, or indeed, any field. The path may be strewn with discouragement, but armed with the right mindset, success is within reach.

Throughout my book, you'll find a curated list of quotations that have been my guiding stars in this exhilarating journey. Choosing favorites was no easy task, but I hope these words inspire you as much as they have inspired me.

Live at Nine was more than a show; it was a crucible, a stage that honed my skills and bolstered my confidence in front of the camera. The community's warm reception and their endearing references to me as a 'local celebrity' were affirmations of my growth. I am forever grateful to Woody Seymour for opening this door of opportunity.

As the years rolled by, my recognition within the community grew. My journey with *Live at Nine* spanned an enriching eleven years. My final act as a co-host unfolded on September 28, 2009, with Jim Dilettoso as our esteemed guest. A chance introduction by Lance Britt, a fellow entertainment industry professional, led to this encounter with one of the most versatile and talented individuals I've had the pleasure to meet.

Jim Dilettoso, a producer and innovator with over four decades of experience in technology and media, has left indelible marks on various fields. From developing cutting-edge gadgets for major rock tours and broadcast TV to advising Shirley MacLaine, *Arizona State University*, and the U.S. Olympics, his contributions are vast and varied. His appearances on numerous TV shows, discussing his research on the paranormal and Unidentified Flying Objects (UFOs), are a testament to his diverse interests and expertise.

Bidding adieu to *Live at Nine* was a bittersweet moment; however, having Jim Dilettoso as my final live interview was a fitting finale to this chapter of my life. His inspiring journey served as a reminder of the endless possibilities that lay ahead, fueling my resolve to continue exploring the captivating world of entertainment.

As my journey with *Live at Nine* drew to a close, I found myself at the crossroads of burgeoning opportunities and the relentless march of time. My aspirations were expanding, my horizons broadening, and the clock was ticking. To realize my career goals, I had to embrace change, to step beyond the familiar.

The specter of public speaking had almost deterred me from this journey, but I chose to persevere. This experience underscored a universal truth - success and fulfillment often lie on the other side of fear. Each experience, each gig, is a passage, a lesson to be carried forward.

A year later, in September 2010, I found myself back on the set of *Live at Nine* for a special edition show. Reuniting with Woody Seymour, we welcomed JD Demers and his daughter Roxanna to discuss their TV series, *The Rusty Bucket Kids Show*. As a recurring character on the series, this was a delightful opportunity to delve into the educational aspects of the show. The camaraderie and shared passion for storytelling made this experience a memorable one.

AUTHOR'S NOTATIONS

Facing your fears 'head on' comes to mind when sharing this chapter about my new experience as a co-host on live television. Growth as mentioned in the quote at the chapter close is an important skill in our development in most professions.

Co-hosting this show helped me to grow and develop, not only in learning new skills but also in developing a newfound confidence in myself. I am glad I didn't play it safely and take the easy way out. It is difficult to face your fears, but that's how dreams blossom and become reality.

ACTOR TRAINING INSIGHTS & TIDBITS

Key Points To Consider

1. **Think about this quote in reference to this chapter on *Live at Nine*.**

   "What if that One thing you're afraid of is the One thing you need to get Your Big Breakthrough and Go to The Next Level?"

   —Jeanette Coron

2. **Learning interview skills for hosting a talk show.**

   Using open-ended questions is especially good for beginning the interview. Being a good listener and conversationalist surely helps also.

3. **Observe interviewing styles of other hosts on television.**

   This is a good way to learn.

4. Work and have fun! Our attitude is everything! Relax and exude confidence.

With Roxana Demers, Woody Seymour (Host) and John Demers on the set of Live at Nine.

"Make a promise to yourself that you will always choose growth over safe and dreams over fear."
Trade Secrets
Releasing 2026
www.donnaink.shop
www.donnaink.net

"In any given moment, we have two options: to step forward into growth or step back into safety."
Trade Secrets
Releasing 2026
www.donnaink.shop
www.donnaink.net

CHAPTER FIVE

SAVED BY TELEVISION

Five months post my special appearance on *Live at Nine*, the universe conspired to offer me a role in *The Rage: Carrie 2* (1999), a sequel to the 1976 cult classic *Carrie*, inspired by a Stephen King novel. The two-day shoot in Charlotte was a whirlwind of experiences, with stars like Emily Bergl, Jason London, Amy Irving, and Dylan Bruno sharing the set.

The first day, I found myself in the holding area, the backstage haven for extras, awaiting my call to the set. My husband, Danny, was my steadfast companion during this journey. As the day drew to a close, an offhand comment by the casting assistant about needing another male extra for the following day caught my attention. I turned to Danny, offering him a chance to step into the limelight. With a touch of reluctance, he agreed, deciding to seize the opportunity to experience the magic of filmmaking firsthand.

The following day, we found ourselves on set, amidst the transformed corridors of *Johnson C. Smith University* in Charlotte, North Carolina. The university had metamorphosed into a mental hospital for our scene. I was cast as a mental patient, confined to a wheelchair, positioned strategically behind the female lead, Emily Bergl. Danny, on the other hand, was to play the role of a visitor, standing beside none other than Amy Irving. This was our moment under the spotlight, a testament to the unpredictable and exhilarating journey that is the *World Of Entertainment*.

Amy Irving, the star of the show, was cordial with Danny and another gentleman nearby. However, when it came to me, it was a different story. She seemed oblivious to my presence. I couldn't help but notice a certain preference for the male company, which, to be fair, was understandable! Danny had indeed chosen an opportune day to step into the world of film-making.

The film itself was a hotbed of intrigue from the get-go. Rumors swirled about a major shakeup in the crew, with key roles such as the Director and Assistant Director being replaced. The whispers on set suggested that the reins had been handed over to women. There were also murmurs about a significant portion of the previously shot footage being discarded, although the veracity of this claim remained uncertain. This behind-the-scenes drama added an extra layer of intrigue to the entire experience.

With the completion of *The Rage: Carrie 2*, the stage was set for its grand unveiling. My talent agent in Durham, recognizing the significant contribution of her clients to the film, orchestrated a premiere celebration at a local theater. As my husband and I nestled into our seats, anticipation bubbled within us. The prospect of seeing ourselves on the silver screen was exhilarating.

I was certain that my scene with the star, seated in a wheelchair right behind her, would secure my screen presence. This belief was further cemented when a crew member noted down my name and that of my wheelchair pusher. However, as the mental ward scene unfolded, my on-screen avatar was conspicuously absent. The disappointment was crushing.

In a twist of fate, my husband, who had accompanied me on a whim, made not one, but two appearances in the background. His debut on the big screen was a source of amusement for us, especially considering his initial reluctance to join the industry. His complaints about the 'hurry up and wait' nature of the business and the endless sitting around, reminiscent of his military days, did nothing to dampen my enthusiasm.

As we exited the premiere, my disappointment was palpable. But as fate would have it, Linda Loveland from TV

Channel 5 and *Fox 50* approached me for an interview about the premiere. Wiping away my tears, I agreed. The next morning, an excited call from an acquaintance brought the news of my appearance on the morning news. Although I missed seeing myself on air, knowing I had made it to the screen, albeit the smaller one was a consolation.

Danny and I shared many laughs over his unexpected screen debut. His colleagues at work even presented him with a framed picture of himself inside a star, a creative gesture by his administrative assistant. Despite the rollercoaster of emotions, the experience was a valuable lesson in the unpredictable and exciting world of entertainment.

AUTHOR'S NOTATIONS

It is important to learn and *take away* learned wisdom from each experience we have. Be prepared for the unexpected. Know that disappointments can and do happen but also do exciting opportunities. The exciting opportunity may not always be for you, but for another family member or friend. Be happy for them and share in their opportunity. Your good attitude will rebound on you and reward you in the future.

ACTOR TRAINING INSIGHTS & TIDBITS

Key Points To Consider

A lesson to learn early on even though you were filmed while doing a scene doesn't always mean that you will appear in the movie. The producers may need to cut scenes in order to meet a certain time frame. If the scene isn't critical to the storyline your scene may be edited out. Disappointing but true as you will see from my experiences.

We can look for opportunity or success in one direction and it comes to us from another direction. Look at the turn of events I had in my film experience in this chapter. I was edited out from the film but then was interviewed on TV. My viewing audience was more likely greater on TV than the movie.

TRADE SECRETS

Walking Among the Stars

A Memoir & Manual of My Career Experience

Catherine Rogers Sewell

REAL TIME
ROADMAP TO ACTING

CATHERINE SEWELL

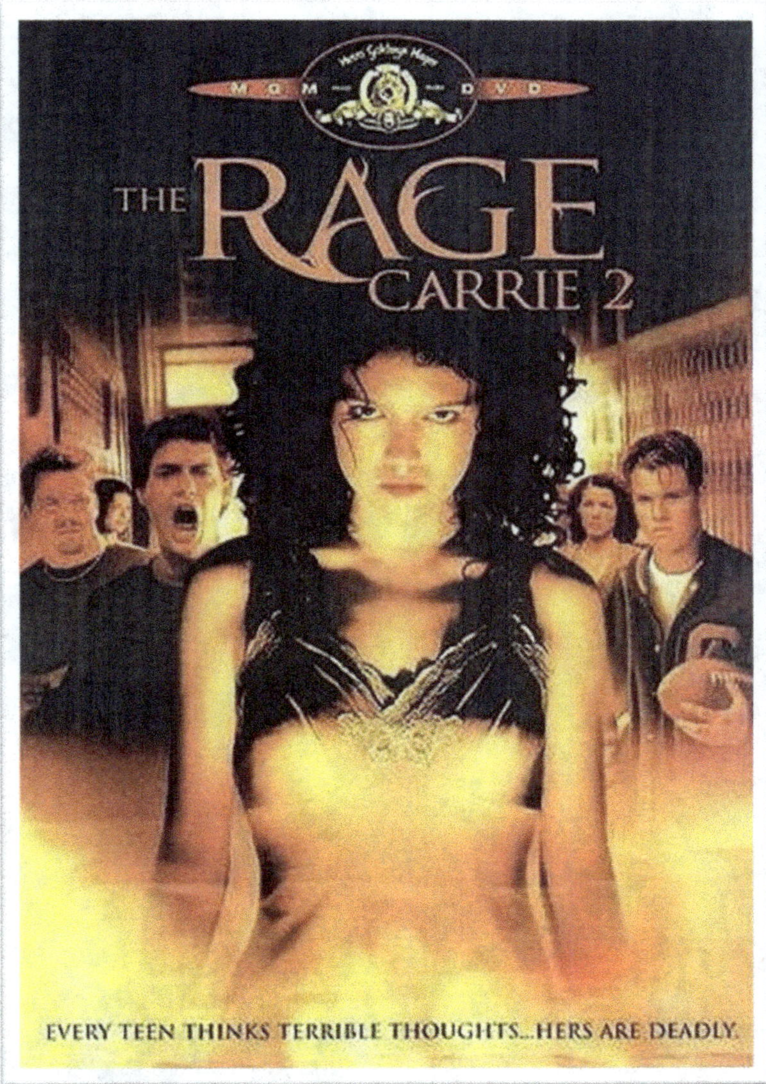
MGM DVD
THE RAGE
CARRIE 2
EVERY TEEN THINKS TERRIBLE THOUGHTS...HERS ARE DEADLY.

"If you do not expect the unexpected, you will not find it, for it is not to be reached by search or trail."
Trade Secrets
www.donnaink.shop
www.donnaink.net

"Self-confidence is the first requisite to great understandings."
Trade Secrets
www.donnaink.shop
www.donnaink.net

CHAPTER SIX

FIRST COMMERCIALS & NEXT FILM

In the summer of 1998, my journey in the world of commercials began. My Durham talent agent presented me with an opportunity to be an extra in a commercial for *UNC Healthcare*. This was my initiation into the world of 'stand' commercials, where extras fill the bleachers of a football field or racetrack. The experience was a baptism by fire, quite literally, as we braved the sweltering heat, yearning for the respite of air conditioning and the refreshment of cold water. Despite the challenging conditions, we were all hopeful actors, eager to leave our mark. This was the first of many *stand* commercials that would dot my career path.

The very next commercial, which happened in the same week, was a delightful departure from the norm. I found myself donning the guise of a pink flamingo. This opportunity came from an independent filmmaker in Laurinburg, North Carolina, who was creating low-budget commercials. He crafted flamingo masks for his daughter and me, and we pranced around a car lot, striking flamingo poses by different cars, all while clad in pink attire. This experience, though unpaid, was invaluable in terms of the exposure and experience it offered.

My mother, who lived near Laurinburg, had access to the commercials on her local stations. However, she was initially embarrassed to acknowledge my participation in these early commercials. The repeated airing of the commercials didn't help matters. However, as my career progressed and the qual-

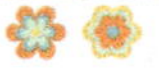

ity of my commercials improved, she gradually came to accept and appreciate my work.

Today, these early commercials serve as a source of amusement for me and my friends. They remind us of the humble beginnings, the initial struggles, and the journey that has led me to where I am today. They are a testament to the fact that every step, no matter how small or seemingly ridiculous, contributes to the larger journey of growth and success.

In that same transformative year, I was presented with an opportunity to be part of a major film - *Bruno*, directed by the legendary Shirley MacLaine. The star-studded cast included Alex Linz, Kathy Bates, and MacLaine herself. My call to action arrived on a day of filming in Raleigh, North Carolina, a location that was conveniently close to home.

The setting was the iconic *Memorial Auditorium Building* in downtown Raleigh; its facade temporarily masked to represent a school for a scene in the movie. Under the relentless sun, I embraced the role of a religious protestor, fervently waving a Bible behind the formidable figure of Shirley MacLaine. Yes, you can spot me in the film, a fervent figure trailing behind MacLaine, Bible in hand.

Working on films offers a fascinating window into the dynamics of the cast and crew. Stacey Halprin, who portrayed Bruno's mother, was rumored to have been discovered by MacLaine on the *Oprah Show*. While the authenticity of this tale remains uncertain, it adds an intriguing layer to the narrative. Alex D. Linz, the young actor who played Bruno, was a bundle of energy, his playful antics occasionally earning him a gentle reminder from MacLaine to focus on the task at hand.

One memorable incident was a heated argument between two crew members about a particular segment of the film. MacLaine, upon overhearing the dispute, intervened with a firm command to cease the argument. This moment served as a stark reminder of the passion and intensity that underpins the world of filmmaking.

MacLaine, it seemed, had little patience for discord on set, a sentiment I could empathize with. Following that scene, we relocated to another downtown building. Alongside other extras, I found myself perched on the building's steps, awaiting my call to action.

Observing MacLaine was an education in itself. I watched as she navigated the set, her voice echoing through the halls as she called for her wig. She ascended the stairs, passing me by, then descended, all the while engrossed in her tasks. I held my tongue, resisting the urge to engage her in conversation. We were advised not to interact with the stars or the director while on set, a rule I adhered to. MacLaine, wearing both the hats of a director and an actress, was undoubtedly swamped. Any interruption could potentially disrupt her focus.

Despite not being called for that particular scene, the day was far from a loss. It concluded, leaving behind a treasure trove of memories and experiences, each one a stepping-stone in my journey in the world of acting..

AUTHOR'S NOTATIONS

The advantage of trying different experiences is to see what you enjoy doing and what you don't like. I found out fairly quickly that the *stands* extra work wasn't for me. I tolerated working on several of these but decided after gathering all the learning and experience from it, to move on to new opportunities.

The film experience in the chapter showed me the importance of teamwork and trying to get along with your fellow workers.

ACTOR TRAINING INSIGHTS & TIDBITS

Key Points To Consider

Ensure you know the correct filming date and your call time (the time that you need to arrive on set). Generally, you will receive your call time by eMail the day before in the late afternoon.

Find out what wardrobe or any hair or makeup preparations you will be asked to bring to the shoot.

Find out the contact information of the person who booked you in case you are unable to work for some reason and need to inform them.

Be sure of where you will be shooting and what transporttation you will need. Find out who the person is from production that you need to report to. Should you run late to set, you should call this contact person and let them know.

Find out about parking. You are responsible for any fees you have to pay. Most sets provide parking space for you.

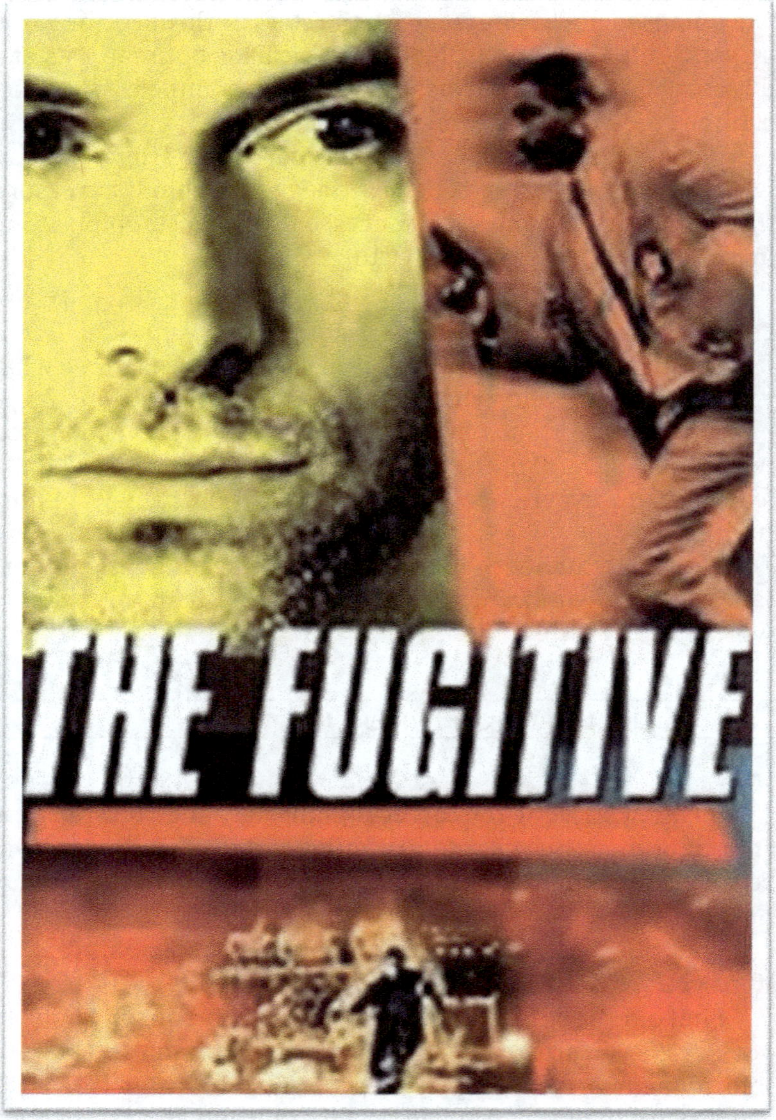

Bruno, directed by the legendary Shirley MacLaine – my first film.

"Creativity is thinking up new things.
Innovation is doing new things."
—Theodore Levitt
Trade Secrets
by
Catherine Sewell
Releasing 2026
www.donnaink.shop
www.donnaink.net
CATHERINE SEWELL
TRADE SECRETS

"The hallmark of successful people
is that they are always stretching
themselves to learn new things."
—Carol D Dweck
Trade Secrets
by
Catherine Sewell
Releasing 2026
www.donnaink.shop
www.donnaink.net
CATHERINE SEWELL
TRADE SECRETS

CHAPTER SEVEN

1998 CONTINUES WITH DAWSON'S CREEK

In the autumn of 1998, I found myself stepping onto the set of *Dawson's Creek*, a golden opportunity presented to me by *Fincannon & Associates*. The details of my debut episode elude me, but the thrill and joy of the experience remain vivid in my memory. My journey with the show spanned from 2000 to 2001, each episode a new adventure.

One such adventure was an episode where I invited my niece, a fan of the show, to join me. Our set for the day was the picturesque *Riverfront Walk on Water Street* in downtown Wilmington. As the day melted into a cool evening, the sight of the river under the night sky was a spectacle to behold.

That day, we were treated to a taste of stardom. As we waited for our scene, a caterer approached us with a platter of snacks. Standing there, being served amidst the hustle and bustle of the set, we felt like true *big shots*. The bystanders, engrossed in the filming, seemed to share this sentiment.

The episode turned out to be an all-nighter, but the excitement kept our spirits high. When it aired, we caught a glimpse of my niece walking down the street behind the actors. In a twist of fate, I found myself upstaged by a family member once again, much like in *Carrie II* when my husband stole the limelight. But as an extra, one knows that the chances of being seen are slim. Spotting a sliver of my back in the scene was a small victory. Seeing my niece enjoy her first and last foray into the business was the real reward. Now a busy pharmacist, she's

certainly earning more than an extra, but the memories of that day are priceless.

Another chapter in my *Dawson's Creek* journey unfolded with a wedding scene. The day was filled with joy and excitement as I was cast as a wedding guest, an observer of the beautiful ceremony. If you know where to look, you can spot me in the crowd. The festivities continued as I was paired with another extra for a dance sequence near the newlyweds. Clad in a pink suit, I twirled and swayed on the stage, a distant figure in the grand celebration.

Joshua Jackson, one of the stars of the show, was a constant source of amusement, his playful antics and jovial demeanor lighting up the set. Despite his youth, he exuded a sense of maturity that was quite endearing.

As the day progressed, an unexpected encounter took me by surprise. In between takes, the director approached me and we shared a spontaneous dance. The surprise left me in a state of shock, and in a playful jest, I quipped aloud, "He must be drunk," implying that only inebriation could lead him to dance with me. I hoped he took it in the spirit of humor it was intended. The Director, known to us only as Jim, had chosen to dance with me, a moment that was both thrilling and memorable.

Upon watching the episode, I discovered that our dance sequence, positioned right behind the lead couple, had been left on the cutting room floor. Despite this, the memory of that day, the laughter, the dance, and the unexpected encounter with Jim, remains etched in my mind. These experiences, though unseen on screen, were integral to my journey in the world of acting.

Dawson's Creek, with its generous budget, pulled out all the stops for a wedding scene. A real wedding cake, a lavish spread of food under a grand tent, and an array of beautiful flowers set the stage. The production was a massive undertaking, with a large crew working tirelessly to bring the vision to life. The culinary delights on set were a treat, with extras enjoying the same gourmet fare as the stars and crew. The *chuck wagon* was our go-to for the main course, with other tables laden with salads, hot vegetables, and desserts. For couples working as extras, it was a chance to double their earnings and enjoy a sumptuous meal.

After my fifth episode, the balance between the time and money invested in gaining experience and the modest pay of $48.50 a day began to tilt. The commute no longer seemed justifiable, and I decided to step away from the show after 2001. The series concluded in 2003, but I still have my *Dawson's Creek* T-shirt as a memento of my journey.

In 1998, I was juggling my part-time job at a school system with my burgeoning career in the film industry. The financial scales were tipped heavily toward expenses, but I was not in this business solely for the money. The prospect of getting paid was always a bonus, but the real reward was the experience and growth. However, the escalating travel costs and the expense of classes and training prompted me to reassess my approach.

Training is a crucial aspect of an actor's journey; without it, one risks appearing unprepared before professional casting directors, potentially jeopardizing future opportunities. This is a business, and maintaining a professional mindset is essential. I invested heavily in classes during the first four years, and while I now take fewer, the importance of regular training remains paramount. Like any profession, continuous learning is the key to success.

In the early stages of my acting journey, finding workshops in the Carolinas was akin to searching for a needle in a haystack. Fast forward to the present, and the landscape has transformed, with a plethora of workshops, particularly those conducted by casting directors, now readily available.

Casting directors are the gatekeepers of the industry, the crucial link between production companies and talent. They are the ones who bring in potential actors for auditions, shaping the cast of a film. Participating in their workshops can provide invaluable insights into what they seek in auditions. Many of them bring a wealth of experience to the table, with some having treaded the path of an actor before transitioning into casting.

Parallel to formal training, working on independent films can be an equally enriching learning experience. It's a hands-on approach where trial and error serve as your tutors. I strive to diversify my roles as much as possible, each character offering unique lessons and growth opportunities. However, in North

Carolina, the scope for choice is limited. Auditions are dictated by what's available within your age range and type.

When compared to states like Louisiana or Texas, let alone the traditional hubs of Los Angeles and New York, opportunities in North Carolina can seem sparse. However, the advent of state film incentives is reshaping the industry landscape, influencing filmmakers' choice of location. The world of film and television is ever-evolving, and staying adaptable is key to navigating its dynamic currents.

In the realm of film production, financial prudence often dictates the choice of location. States like Louisiana, Georgia, and Texas have emerged as attractive destinations in the past decade, thanks to their lucrative tax incentives. I once playfully suggested to my husband that we consider relocating to one of these states, but the idea was met with a firm no.

For some actors, particularly those unencumbered by familial obligations, the prospect of moving to states with more opportunities is enticing. The thought of relocating to bustling metropolises like Los Angeles or New York can be daunting, especially for someone like me, who hails from a small town. While Los Angeles is the Mecca for film, New York City is the heart of theater. The competition in these cities is fierce, unlike the relatively less competitive southern states.

I've always maintained that if I were to *make it* - however one chooses to define that - it would be right here in North Carolina. My suggestion of moving was merely a tease aimed at my husband. Yet, during slower times, I confess that the thought has crossed my mind. When the acting bug bites, the desire to perform is all-consuming. It's a sentiment shared by many of my friends in the industry. The relentless pursuit of the next gig, the constant yearning to be on stage or in front of the camera, can be likened to an addiction of sorts. But it's this very passion that fuels our dreams and propels us forward in this exciting world of acting.

AUTHOR'S NOTATIONS

Though working on films and television shoots share similarities, there are some differences. When you work on a continuing TV series, you will work with the same leads/stars each time. The show will also employ supporting roles and day players that may only work one day. With film, you work with many of the same people until the filming is over in a matter of weeks, months and in some cases a year or more. As I did in Dawson's Creek, it is fun to work on the same series over a period of time. Some series can continue for years if popular and sponsored well.

ACTOR TRAINING INSIGHTS & TIDBITS

Key Points To Consider

1. Display respect and courteousness to all.
2. Dress appropriately for the projects.
3. Be kind and friendly to all.
4. Always be on time.
5. Be helpful when appropriate.
6. Follow instructions from the crew. An Assistant Director (AD) will be assigned to the extras / background Actors.
7. Be open to any feedback or instructions given to you by the Director or Assistant Director or other crew.
8. The crew should go first in the "chow" line. They are served first and then the extras.
9. Silence your cellphone.
10. Quiet on set when instructed to be.
11. Don't try to talk with the Principal Actors. They need to concentrate on their performance.
12. Be careful on set as there is a lot of equipment and chords running everywhere. Be mindful of the things around you.
13. Pay attention to detail and continuity in the movements or actions you are asked to do by the Director while filming. Listen carefully to any instructions.
14. Please don't complain on set.
15. Be patient, setup takes time-lighting, sound, camera, etc.

16. Don't just decide to leave set for the day. This could cause an issue in continuity in the scenes.
17. No drugs or alcohol on set.
18. Before you leave for the day, be sure to return any props or wardrobe you were given to use.

CHAPTER EIGHT

WORK IN THE YEAR OF 1999

The year 1999 marked a significant uptick in my acting journey compared to 1998, though my roles were primarily as an extra in films and commercials. A notable milestone was my first involvement in a television movie, *Having Her Say: The Delany Sisters' First 100 Years.* This poignant narrative revolved around the lives of Sadie and Bessie Delany, two African-American sisters who defied the odds to live past 100. Raised on a North Carolina farm, they navigated the hurdles of racism to carve out successful careers in New York City - Sadie as the city's first African-American home-economics teacher, and Bessie as its second African-American dentist.

The film boasted a stellar cast, with Ruby Dee portraying Bessie and Diahann Carroll stepping into the shoes of Sadie. Carroll's transformation for the role was so convincing I barely recognized her. The ensemble also included renowned actors like Della Reese, Richard Roundtree, Amy Madigan, and Lisa Anderson, whose beauty left a lasting impression on me.

One of the highlights of the experience was seeing Camille O. Cosby, Bill Cosby's wife. Listed as the executive producer on the *International Movie Database (IMDB),* her active involvement in the filming process gave the impression of her being the director. My husband joined me as an extra for both days of filming, and to our surprise, we were provided with a trailer - a luxury seldom afforded to extras. This unexpected perk added a dash of excitement to our experience.

The filming took place in Gastonia and Salisbury, near Charlotte, North Carolina. Despite the long hours and the demanding nature of the work, the thrill of being part of such a meaningful project made every moment worthwhile.

Early in my acting journey, I discovered an unspoken rule of film wardrobes - if you're above a size 12, finding a fitting costume can be a challenge. I recall a day on set when a fellow extra, a woman of larger size, grappled with this reality. Her frustration was palpable as the wardrobe department struggled to find a suitable outfit for her. That day, the usually well-oiled machine of a film set seemed to falter in its rhythm.

Once we were finally attired in period costumes, hair and make-up impeccably done, our scene had concluded. Our role was simple - to stand near a train, embodying the essence of passengers from a bygone era. The backdrop for this scene was the historic railroad station in Salisbury. One of the perks of this profession is the opportunity to explore new places, and this TV movie was my ticket to Salisbury, a city I might never have visited otherwise.

Shortly after this experience, another TV opportunity surfaced - a pilot for a show called Brookfield. In the TV world, a pilot is a test episode, a pitch to networks in the hope of securing a series deal. I spent a day on this project, stepping into the shoes of a professor seated on stage, right behind two of the lead actors delivering a speech at the podium. Despite my prime position, the uncertainty of the pilot being picked up for a series, and the whims of the editing room, meant that my on-screen appearance was far from guaranteed. But such is the nature of the business – unpredictable, yet endlessly exciting.

The spring and summer of 1999 marked a vibrant chapter in my acting journey. I found myself immersed in regional commercials and independent films, embracing the role of an extra with gusto. My second foray into regional commercials, which cater to specific television viewing areas, was a valuable addition to my growing repertoire.

One of the independent films, aptly titled Clowns, offered a unique experience. My husband and I were cast together, our faces painted to resemble clowns. Exhausted but exhilarated after a day of filming, we decided to forego the makeup removal and embarked on a comical drive home, our clown visages drawing amused glances from fellow motorists.

The other film, initially titled *Morning*, was a local production by *Down Home Entertainment*, based in High Point, North Carolina. The film was later renamed *A Touch of Fate*, a common occurrence in industry. Teri Hatcher, who would later gain fame in *Desperate Housewives*, was part of the cast.

The highlight of working on this film was the friendships I forged, particularly with two seasoned male actors. One of them, Robert Harris, became a dear friend, a confidante, and a source of encouragement. After a lifetime in theater, Robert earned his *Screen Actors Guild (SAG)* eligibility at the age of 72, thanks to his memorable role as a storekeeper in the feature film *Cabin Fever*. His success, which included gracing the cover of *The Hollywood Reporter*, was a testament to the rewards of hard work and perseverance.

Despite his advancing years, Robert's passion for acting remained undiminished. He continued to attend film festivals and events, signing autographs and accepting roles until the final months of his life. Robert passed away on July 25, 2015, at the age of eighty-five. His absence is deeply felt, and our conversations are dearly missed. The acting community lost not just a talented actor, but a wonderful human being. His legacy serves as a reminder that success in acting, as in any profession, is a blend of passion, perseverance, and the courage to seize opportunities.

In the unpredictable world of acting, having a confidant who understands the nuances of the industry can be a lifeline. Robert was that friend for me, a beacon of encouragement who could lift my spirits during the inevitable lows. The allure, the challenges, and the exhilarating highs of the entertainment business are best understood by those who have experienced them firsthand. Friends outside the industry, while well-meaning, often see only successes, oblivious to the hard work and sacrifices that pave the path to achievement.

My circle of friends and acquaintances have always been supportive, their excitement palpable when I land a role in a project they can watch. Family, on the other hand, can sometimes struggle to understand the intricacies of this career choice. Fear often fuels their discouragement - fear of rejection, fear of the time it takes to make progress, and fear fueled by the cautionary tales of some celebrities' lives.

However, at the heart of any successful career is an inherent passion. Doing what we love brings a sense of fulfillment that outweighs the hard work and challenges. It infuses our journey with joy, making every step, every sacrifice, worth it..

AUTHOR'S NOTATIONS

The quotes in this chapter confirm for me the importance of passion in our work; as I am happier doing what I enjoy and don't mind working hard to reach my goals. An earlier agent of mine used an inspirational quote at the end of all her e-mails and it made an impression on me.

Having a passion for your work along with training and hard work does make for a great combination in reaching your goals. If you don't begin by loving what you do, then the process may be more difficult and lacking in enjoyment and fulfillment.

ACTOR TRAINING INSIGHTS & TIDBITS

Key Points To Consider

1. If you are doing extra work and are a female requiring a wardrobe fitting, know that you may have difficulty being fitted for plus sizes, especially period pieces. Most of any original period piece wardrobe is in smaller sizes.

2. Enjoy meeting other Actors and crew on set as you may meet lifelong friends. This is important for support in this very competitive business. Also, you can meet some surprisingly very interesting and highly educated and trained individuals who like to perform extra work as a diversion. Example: I met a nuclear physicist that designed some highly sophisticated medical equipment in one of the top North Carolina universities.

3. Be kind and friendly to all you meet. You never know who you may be talking to or communicating with in this business. Let them remember you for that smile rather than that complaint!

Poignant narrative revolved around the lives of Sadie and Bessie Delany, two African-American sisters who defied the odds to live past 100.

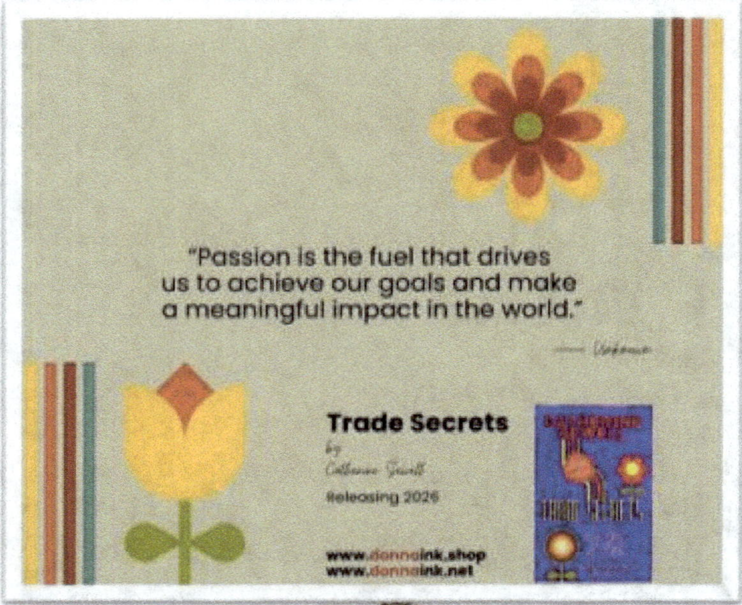
"Passion is the fuel that drives
us to achieve our goals and make
a meaningful impact in the world."
Trade Secrets
Releasing 2026
www.donnaink.shop
www.donnaink.net

"Nothing great in the world has ever been
accomplished without passion."
Trade Secrets
Releasing 2026
www.donnaink.shop
www.donnaink.net

CHAPTER NINE

TURN OF THE CENTURY

As we ushered in the new millennium in 2000, my acting journey took an exciting turn. I landed a role as the spokesperson for a regional commercial aired on cable, promoting a chiropractic center. The commercial, which aired extensively in the Fayetteville area, marked a significant milestone in my career. However, when I revisit it now, I can't help but cringe at my pronounced Southern accent, a stark contrast to the Standard English accent I was striving to master. It's amusing to reflect on how far I've come since then!

That year also saw me stepping into the shoes of an extra for a regional network commercial and the TV series *The Fugitive*. When my agent called me for a two-day shoot in Savannah, Georgia, I jumped at the opportunity. Despite the modest pay, the prospect of working on *The Fugitive* was too enticing to resist. My friend, Renee Bollten (now Vesci), and I made the long drive to Savannah, a charming coastal city we had the pleasure of exploring by night.

One of the highlights of this project was a chance encounter with the star of the show, Tim Daly, who portrayed Dr. Richard Kimble. During a scene, as he was running and I was walking, he accidentally brushed past me. He paused to check if I was alright before continuing his run. This was my second 'up close' encounter with him. The first was on our arrival day in Savannah when we ran into him at the production office. Dressed casually in jeans and a T-shirt, he was the epitome of an approachable 'movie star'. These encounters, though fleeting, left a lasting impression and added a dash of starstruck excitement to the experience.

My unexpected encounters with Tim Daly certainly made for an exciting tale to share back home. I had not one, but two memorable *run-ins* with him. However, in the whirlwind of filming, I forgot to note the air date of the episode and missed it. Another actor mentioned not spotting me in the episode, which wasn't surprising. After all, the *run-in* accident probably didn't make the final cut!

In 2000, I had the pleasure of working on a major film, *Summer Catch*, featuring a star-studded cast that included Freddie Prinze, Jr., Jessica Biel, Fred Ward, and Brittany Murphy. My friend Renee, who had accompanied me to Savannah, joined me again for this project in Beaufort, North Carolina. The fascinating thing about Renee is that she's now my talent agent at *Fast Lane Talent* in Charlotte. It's a testament to the dynamic nature of this industry - one day you're an actor, the next you could be a Producer, Director, or Talent Agent.

Our filming schedule spanned afternoons and evenings, set against the backdrop of a full-fledged baseball field constructed on a woman's property. The field, built to professional standards or close to it, must have been a significant investment. I heard once the filming was wrapped up, the homeowner had the field dismantled and the property restored to its original state. While it seemed like a waste to me, I understood that everyone has their preferences. I couldn't help but think that the community could have benefited from such a well-equipped field, complete with a ticket booth and bleachers. But such are the intricacies of the film world - a constant dance of creation and deconstruction.

This was one Hollywood film, in addition to Bruno, you can see me in, if you know where to look. You can spot me in the crowd, engaged in conversation with a friend, right behind Fred Ward who is enjoying a beer under a large oak tree. We were all engrossed in a baseball game featuring Freddie Prinze, Jr. Our holding area, the place where we waited for our call to the set, was uniquely located near an old cemetery, under the shadow of towering oak trees. Despite the lack of nearby buildings for us to take shelter in, the ball field was so well lit that it seemed as if we were filming in broad daylight rather than in the dead of night. Such is the magic of the movies!

The highlight of that year was landing a small speaking role in an independent film titled *Sun's Last Days*. This was a significant milestone for me, as I had been auditioning for speaking roles without success. Independent films, often produced on shoestring budgets compared to their Hollywood counterparts, offer a unique platform for filmmakers to bring their vision to life. They have been the launch pad for many successful Christian films and provide invaluable on-set experience for actors. They also offer writers and producers the freedom to express their views and interests. Despite the financial constraints, the creative fulfillment that independent films offer is truly priceless.

The year 2000 marked a significant milestone in my acting journey. I landed a speaking role in *Sun's Last Days*, where I portrayed a parole officer. The cast convened for a meeting to discuss the film, and soon after, I received the call to shoot my part. With a mix of anticipation and nerves, I arrived on set in Durham, ready to give my best performance. This was my first speaking role, and I was determined to make it count. The experience went smoothly, and I left the set with a sense of accomplishment and a valuable addition to my resume.

The camaraderie on set was palpable, and any initial anxieties quickly dissipated. I am eternally grateful to the production team of *Ujamaa Digital Works* for giving me my first speaking role in a film. The premiere was a thrilling experience, and seeing myself on the big screen was a moment of pride.

Soon after, I auditioned for a part in a film titled *Get Out of Here*. Although I didn't land the role I auditioned for, I was cast as a featured extra. The film was aired multiple times on *NC Visions*, a show on the *University of North Carolina Center for Public Television (UNC-TV)*. To my surprise, people still recognize me from the show, a testament to the impact even an extra can have.

As the century turned, I found myself involved in an independent film, the title of which I'm hesitant to mention. In hindsight, I realize I should have gleaned more about the film from its title. To compound matters, I roped in my husband to join me as an extra. When we realized the true nature of the film, we regretted our decision to participate. But such is the nature of the acting world - it's a constant learning experience, filled with unexpected twists and turns.

As the action unfolded on set, we instinctively moved away from the camera's gaze. In a profession where visibility is often coveted, we found ourselves hoping to remain unseen in this particular film. The late-night shoot stretched into the early hours of the morning, and the drive home was marked by a palpable silence. The next day brought an unexpected call from production - they wanted me to consider a speaking part. The prospect was enticing, but the script they sent left me speechless, and not in a good way. The words assigned to my character were ones I couldn't bring myself to utter. I expressed my reservations to the Assistant Director, who graciously understood my stance.

Later, my agent informed us that we could request to have our names included in the credits. This was one occasion where I chose to forgo that privilege. The film, available on DVD and Pay Per View, was something I only dared to watch years later. To my surprise, we were visible in a few scenes. The experience served as a reminder to be cautious about the projects I choose, as one might end up being seen in unexpected ways. The film, despite its suggestive title, turned out to be more humorous than provocative. The editing process had transformed it; even omitting the speaking role I was initially offered. It was a stark reminder of the old adage, "You can't always judge a book by its cover."

Now, I'm sure you're curious about the name of this film. Well, brace yourself. The film was titled *Ding-A-Ling Less*. Quite a title to stir the imagination, wouldn't you agree?

In the year 2000, I had the privilege of securing a speaking role with the esteemed *North Carolina School of the Arts (NCSA)* in Winston-Salem, North Carolina. One of my aspirations that year was to participate in a student film there, a platform renowned for nurturing future filmmakers. The students at NCSA are privy to top-notch training and state-of-the-art equipment, making it an enriching experience for budding actors like me. Participating in these films often provides us with a copy of our work, a valuable addition to our performance reels. A performance reel is a compilation of an actor's work, providing casting directors with a glimpse of their acting prowess. As an actor's career progresses and their body of work expands, a well-curated reel becomes an essential tool for securing future roles. I would highly recommend anyone starting in this industry to seize opportunities to work with NCSA or other film schools for the invaluable training they offer. I had the opportunity to work on five student films, one of which found a place on my performance reel.

Over the years, I've been a part of numerous films and commercials, many of which I've never seen. As an extra, visibility is often elusive, though there are exceptions. Your chances of being seen increase if you're designated as a featured extra at the outset, as was the case with the student film I mentioned earlier. However, even in major Hollywood productions, landing a role as a featured extra can be challenging. I've known actors who were cast in speaking roles, only to have their parts edited out.

Even when you secure a role, film it, and receive your paycheck, the suspense lingers until you see the final product on the big screen. The editing block can be a ruthless arbiter of an actor's fate. So, if you decide to embark on this thrilling journey, take a leaf out of my book - refrain from announcing your appearance until you've seen the final product. That said, those rare moments when you are featured or manage to snag some screen time can be incredibly rewarding, providing just the right amount of motivation to keep aspiring actors coming back for more.

AUTHOR'S NOTATIONS

Be open-minded and learn from all your experiences, as they do add to your knowledge. On movie sets, which can be a cosmos of life, you will be able to observe a great deal. As John Dewey said, 'Learn by doing.' Ideally, you will combine these life experiences with professional training.

Key Points To Consider

In the realm of film, commercials, and industrials, extras or background talents play a crucial role in enhancing the realism of scenes. Here are some educational insights to help you navigate your journey as an extra more effective:

1. **Understanding Instructions**: Thoroughly read the instructions provided by the Casting Director and adhere to them meticulously.
2. **Location Familiarity**: Ensure you comprehend the directions to the shooting location well in advance. Consider using a map or GPS for guidance. Upon arrival, you'll typically park in the designated area for extras.
3. **Punctuality**: Aim to arrive on time, or better yet early.
4. **Wardrobe Selection**: Bring three to four changes of clothing as recommended. Choose outfits that align with the scene's context. Avoid wearing red, white, or black unless specified otherwise. If the scene is set in a specific period, they might request you to bring suitable attire. If not, they'll usually provide what you need. Remember to know your sizes.
5. **Time Commitment**: Refrain from asking about the shoot's duration. The exact time is often uncertain and depends on how the day progresses. Plan to be there all day, and in many cases for film, it could extend to 12 hours or longer. Avoid asking to leave early as your presence is crucial for the entire day. Leaving while your scene is still being shot could disrupt continuity, jeopardize your chances of being hired again, and result in non-payment.
6. **On-Set Etiquette**: There's usually a separate craft table for extras on set. Unless you're a *SAG-AFTRA Extra* hired as a union actor, stick to the extras' craft table.
7. **Following Directions**: A production Assistant is typically responsible for managing the extras. Pay close attention to their instructions and follow them diligently.

8. **Payment Process**: For *SAG-AFTRA* films, the production Assistant will provide you with a voucher to fill out for payment. Some non-union films may not use vouchers. Always have two forms of ID handy for completing these vouchers, such as a driver's license and social security card. Other forms of ID like a passport or birth certificate are also acceptable. In North Carolina, children under seventeen years of age need a worker's permit. Extras are typically paid minimum wage, but the exact amount depends on the production company.

9. **Wardrobe Selection**: The wardrobe department will assess your attire and the additional clothing options you bring. It's advisable to wear what you believe best fits the scene to avoid changing outfits. However, there may be instances where you'll be required to change for different scenes. If the scene is set in a specific period or if your clothing choices don't align with the wardrobe department's vision, they will provide you with appropriate attire. Remember to bring your voucher to the wardrobe department and leave it with them until you return your clothing or props at the end of the shoot.

10. **Hair and Makeup**: The hair and makeup team may assess your appearance to determine if it's suitable for the scene. They typically won't style your hair or apply makeup unless the scene is a period piece that requires a specific look. For instance, period pieces set in the 1800s often require only face powder.

11. **Sun Protection**: Ensure you wear and carry sunblock when filming outdoors during the summer. High temperatures can lead to significant sunburn, even with the application of strong sunblock. For instance, I once worked on a day when the temperature reached 105 degrees, as indicated by a time / temperature sign on a downtown street.

12. **Set Etiquette**: Refrain from bringing a camera to the set or using your cellphone camera to take pictures of the stars or set unless you have been given permission. Remember to turn off your cellphone when called to set, as you could be dismissed if your phone disrupts filming. Also, avoid asking

the stars for autographs or pictures unless the project allows for it, you have a relationship with the actor, and the production team approves.

13. **Mealtimes**: On the set of a major film, you'll be served lunch or dinner if you're there for 6 hours after the crew call, not your call time. If you're required on set very early in the morning, breakfast is often provided, ranging from a full hot meal to just donuts and coffee. Set protocol dictates the cast and crew eat first since they need to return to the set before you. Once they've finished, you may eat.

14. **Consider the Importance of Time Management**: As an extra, you may find yourself waiting for extended periods. It's beneficial to bring engaging activities such as books, puzzles, or knitting to utilize this time effectively. Understand you may not always be used, or your involvement may be brief. This knowledge can help manage expectations and prevent disappointment.

15. **Understanding On-Set Etiquette**: It's crucial not to bring companions, spouses, or children to the set unless they are also part of the production. This helps maintain a professsional environment and ensures smooth operations.

16. **Post-Workday Procedures**: After your workday concludes, remember to return any borrowed items to the wardrobe department and retrieve your voucher. You'll need to have a production Assistant sign you out on the voucher, which you should keep for your records. Feel free to bid farewell to any acquaintances you've made during the day.

17. **Cancellation Policy**: Avoid cancelling unless it's an emergency. Casting Directors typically require at least 24 hours' notice for cancellations. Last-minute cancellations can result in not being asked to work again, as they often cause significant inconvenience and extra work for the casting team.

18. **Adapting to Change**: The film industry is dynamic, and changes can occur rapidly. You might receive short notice for work, or weather conditions may not affect your sche-

dule as you might expect. Be prepared for potential schedule extensions, such as being asked to return the following day. Your personal belongings, like your car, may also be requested for use in production, which could result in additional compensation.

19. **Financial Responsibility**: Remember, you are responsible for your travel expenses and any accommodation costs if you choose to stay overnight. Weigh the costs against the benefits of participating in production, as sometimes the expenses may exceed your earnings. However, many find the experience and opportunity to see the stars worth the cost.

20. **The Reward**: The most exciting part of being an extra is the chance to see yourself on the big screen. Enjoy the experience, have fun, and hopefully, we'll see you at the movies!

North Carolina School of the Arts – University of North Carolina.

" Life experiences contribute to knowledge."
—Catherine Sewell
Trade Secrets
by
Catherine Sewell
Releasing 2025
www.donnaink.shop
www.donnaink.net

"People with clear, written goals accomplish far more in a shorter period of time than people without them could ever imagine."
—Catherine Sewell
Trade Secrets
by
Catherine Sewell
Releasing 2025
www.donnaink.shop
www.donnaink.net

CHAPTER TEN

ENTER DIVINE SECRETS OF THE YA-YA SISTERHOOD

As the dawn of 2001 broke, I found myself stepping into the vibrant world of independent cinema, taking on small speaking roles and working as an extra. My journey was further enriched by my involvement in the local TV show, *Live at Nine*, where I honed my skills and gained invaluable experience.

In May, a new adventure beckoned. My agent called with an opportunity to work on the feature film *Shallow Hal* in Charlotte. The film starred Gwyneth Paltrow and Jack Black, and it presented an intriguing challenge for Paltrow, who had to don a body suit to portray a larger version of her character for part of the film.

I was cast in two scenes. In one, I was tasked with pacing up and down the sidewalk in front of a building. This scene also featured Paltrow, sans body suit, and it was a thrill to share the set with her. Around the same time, I had a brief encounter with Jack Black as I exited the building while he entered.

Later that day, I was seated at an outdoor table of a downtown restaurant for another scene. Although my presence in this scene was subtle, the experience of co-existing among the stars was exhilarating.

The excitement didn't end there. Later that month, a Casting Director from Wilmington reached out with an offer to be a stand-in for Dame Maggie Smith in *Divine Secrets of the Ya-Ya*

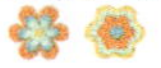

Sisterhood. At the time, I had no idea what a fantastic experience this would turn out to be.

This narrative underscores the unpredictability and excitement of working in the film industry, where every day brings new opportunities and experiences. It's a testament to the power of perseverance, adaptability, and a love for the craft. It also highlights the importance of being prepared for sudden changes and the value of maintaining a professional demeanor on set. Whether you're an aspiring actor or just a film enthusiast, these insights can provide a valuable glimpse into the world of cinema. Enjoy the journey, and who knows? Maybe one day, we'll see you on the big screen!

As the sun rose on my first day of work, I found myself in Faison, North Carolina, stepping onto a bustling film set. To my delight, a familiar face greeted me - a friend who was also working as a stand-in. Her presence added a layer of comfort and camaraderie to the experience.

After signing in, I was ushered to a tent for a hearty breakfast, a small but significant gesture that fuels the day's work. Post-breakfast, I was handed a shirt, its color mirroring the outfit that Maggie Smith, the actor I was standing in for, would be wearing.

For those new to the industry, a stand-in is a crucial part of the filmmaking process. They step in for the actor while the lighting crew, known as grips, adjusts the lighting for each shot. This spares the actor from standing for hours on end during these adjustments. Stand-ins, or Team 2, are usually chosen based on their physical resemblance to the actor they're standing in for, in terms of coloring, hair, and height.

This was a novel experience for me, having only done extra work on major films before. Each day, the assistant director provided us with a script to review, ensuring we were familiar with the day's scenes. Sometimes, stand-ins are asked to read the lines while standing in for lighting adjustments. Despite initial nerves, the thrill of seeing famous stars up close made the experience exhilarating.

Over the course of two months, I worked on this film, with my schedule dictated by Maggie Smith's filming days. Some weeks, I worked one to three days, while towards the end of the film, I worked every day. The intensity of the work schedule meant that for the last couple of weeks, I stayed with a friend in Wilmington, returning home only on weekends.

Working on a film set can be exhausting, with most days stretching to eight to ten hours. The crew, who arrive before and leave after the actors and stand-ins, often work even longer hours. This is why many crew members are young - the demands of the job require stamina and resilience.

Many crew members make significant sacrifices, leaving their families for months at a time to travel to film locations. Despite the hard work and long hours, most persist because of their love for filmmaking. It takes a large and dedicated crew to create a multimillion-dollar film, and stand-ins, as I discovered, are considered an integral part of this crew.

This narrative serves as an educational insight into the world of filmmaking for budding actors, highlighting the importance of resilience, adaptability, and a deep-seated passion for the craft. Remember, every role on a film set, no matter how small, contributes to the magic of the final product.

Stepping onto the set for the first time, I was awestruck by the constellation of stars around me - Maggie Smith, Sandra Bullock, James Garner, Ellen Burstyn, Shirley Knight, and Fionnula Flanagan. Each interaction was a lesson, each observation a masterclass in acting.

Maggie Smith, with her unwavering professionalism, would always express gratitude after I had stood in for her. Her simple "Thank you very much," was a constant reminder of the importance of humility and gratitude in this industry.

Engaging with Shirley Knight and Fionnula Flanagan was a joy. Our conversations were often filled with insights and anecdotes. Shirley shared stories of late bloomers in the industry, reinforcing my belief that it's never too late to pursue your passion. This interaction underscored the importance of perseverance and positivity in an actor's journey.

One day, an actor expressed frustration about a colleague not knowing their lines, causing a delay in production. This incident served as a reality check, highlighting the importance of preparation and professionalism in acting.

Fionnula, struggling to perfect a Southern accent for the word *Atlanta*, received pointers from me. This was a testament to the collaborative nature of acting, where learning and growth are continuous processes.

James Garner, despite his age, amazed me with his dedication and stamina. Some days he would just shuffle along, looking so tired, yet he never faltered. His resilience was a powerful lesson in commitment and passion.

This journey taught me that acting is not just about the glamor and the fame, but also about the hard work, the long hours, and the sacrifices. But when you love what you do, even the most challenging days seem ordinary, and the long hours become a part of the rhythm of life. This is the life of an actor, filled with continuous learning, growth, and unforgettable experiences.

In the bustling world of film, I found myself amidst a constellation of stars. One of them was Mr. Garner, a kind man with a penchant for paperback novels. He would bring a collection to the set, offering them to anyone who wanted one. I took one as a souvenir, a tangible memory of my time on set.

One day, my friend managed to get a picture with Mr. Garner. Unfortunately, I missed my chance as I had stepped away. When I returned, the photo session was over, and he wouldn't pose again. This taught me the importance of seizing opportunities when they present themselves in this fast-paced industry.

Mr. Garner's hair and makeup person often suggested he wear his toupee, but he wasn't too keen on that. This revealed a side of acting that isn't often discussed - the personal choices actors make about their appearance for roles. His passing in 2014 was a great loss to the industry, reminding us of the transient nature of life.

Ellen Burstyn was another star on this film. While I didn't get a chance to converse with her during filming, I was chosen as her foot and leg double for a car scene. This was due to our similar shoe sizes. The wardrobe department was meticulous, evaluating the feet of potential stand-ins. One stand-in was turned down due to a corn on her toe. When it was my turn, I cleverly positioned my foot in the shoe to hide a small bunion under the sandal strap. It worked, and I was accepted.

They prepared my feet for the shoot with a pedicure. During the shoot, I had to be careful to keep my foot positioned so the bunion wouldn't show. It was challenging but rewarding work. I even wore the same gold pants as Ms. Burstyn for the scene. After the shot, they were immediately cleaned for her.

This experience underscored the attention to detail required in film production, from the careful selection of stand-ins to the maintenance of costumes. It also highlighted the importance of adaptability and quick thinking in overcoming challenges. These are valuable lessons for anyone aspiring to make their mark in the world of acting.

In the world of acting, every experience is a lesson, every interaction a story. I found myself in the heart of this world, filming in a gold Rolls Royce, the same one you see Ellen Burstyn driving in the movie. My foot, pressing the brake pedal as Burstyn's character, Vivi, is forced to stop by Teensy (Fionnula Flanagan), made a brief but impactful appearance on the screen.

One day, as I expressed my disappointment to my friend Robert Harris about only my foot being seen in the movie, he quipped, "At least you got your foot in the door." His quick wit brought laughter and a valuable lesson - every opportunity, no matter how small, is a step forward in this industry.

After months of hard work and fun on the film, the journey came to an exciting end with the *Divine Secrets of the Ya-Ya Sisterhood Wrap Party*. With little time to prepare, I found myself buying a dress from Walmart, a reminder that in this industry, it's not always about dressing to impress, but about being present and embracing the moment.

At the party, I was eager to interact with the stars. I found Maggie Smith among the attendees and mustered up the courage to tell her how much I enjoyed being her stand-in. Her response, "Oh, come on now!" I told her that I really did enjoy it and had learned a great deal from observing her. She was lighthearted and friendly, a stark contrast to her professional demeanor on set. This encounter taught me the importance of adaptability and the ability to switch between professional and relaxed environments in the industry.

The most memorable part of our conversation was her parting words, "See you on the big screen." Those words filled me with excitement and hope for my future as an actress, reinforcing the belief that every experience, every role, no matter how small, contributes to one's journey in the world of acting. Maggie Smith graced the screen in the popular television series *Downton Abbey*, a testament to the longevity and versatility a career in acting can offer.

On the final day of filming, an unexpected surprise awaited me and the other stand-ins. Maggie Smith, Shirley Knight, and Fionnula Flanagan had commissioned an artist to create caricatures of themselves in bikinis. Each caricature was signed by the respective actor and even included a personalized note, For *Ya Ya* Catherine. This beautifully matted and framed picture was a testament to the kindness and thoughtfulness of these stars. It was a gift I had never anticipated, a treasure that would forever remind me of the fun times on set with the wonderful crew and actors. This experience underscored the importance of camaraderie and appreciation in the industry. With great sadness, Dame Maggie Smith died on September 27, 2024. She passed away in a London hospital at the age of 89.

Months later, as *Ya-Ya Sisterhood* hit the theatres, I found myself watching the *Oprah Show*. She was interviewing Callie Khouri, the Director, and they showed the scene featuring my foot. Interestingly, the duration of my foot's screen time seemed longer on the show than in the theatrical film. This surprise brought a smile to my face and reminded me of Robert Harris's witty remark about getting my 'foot in the door.' It was a humorous yet profound reminder that every opportunity, no matter how small, contributes to one's journey in the world of acting. My foot, indeed!

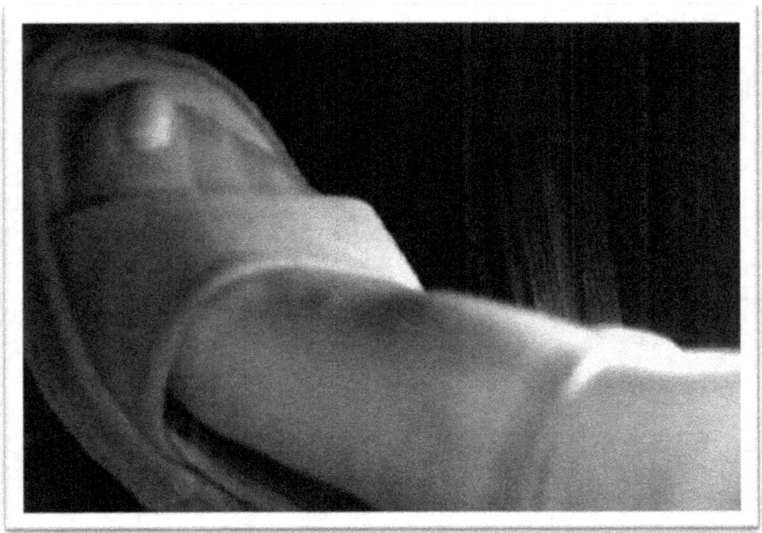

Art Cricature Gift from Maggie Smith, Fionnula Flanagan, and Shirley Knight.

AUTHOR'S NOTATIONS

This chapter included a totally new experience for me in this, my career journey. I was called by an NC Casting Agent to be a stand-in for a major film. I had never done this before. My first response was to research the specifics regarding a stand-in role on set. I was generally familiar with the expectations but wanted to be better prepared. Being more knowledgeable and prepared for a new assignment is critical to your success and confidence. It helps to reduce stress and anxiety when we feel we are prepared.

SUGGESTED LIST OF ACTIVITIES TO HELP YOU REACH YOUR GOALS

This is not an exhaustive list – so, add your own ideas and activities to personalize the following to meet your situation.

1. Read a book, industry magazines, or articles related to your interests and goals.
2. Read a script and practice memorizing the lines.
3. Take an acting, voiceover, drama, etc. class.
4. Network with other Actors. Join acting associations or groups. Attend events such as acting showcases.
5. Look at media sites such as YouTube for acting tips and lessons by trained professional Actors or trainers.
6. Watch a TV show/movie and observe the acting techniques and approaches used.
7. Attend industry parties and events.
8. Schedule a private consultation with a professional acting coach.
9. Meet with your Agent and ask about ways to become more marketable.
10. Schedule a new headshot if it is older than a year or two and especially if you have changed your look.

11. Collect clips from your film work so you can have a reel for Casting Directors to view. Reels do not have to be over a minute or two long. You can also have separate ones for varied film categories, such as drama, comedy, horror, suspense, etc.
12. You can purchase equipment for video filming your own auditions or hire someone to film you. Many actors today use their cell phones. Video recording our own auditions has eliminated the need for in-person auditions, which saves time, money, and stress.
13. Some independent films may have you send the audition directly to them. Few auditions are done in person now. Even most callbacks are virtual.
14. Join any scene study groups you can find. Another option is to team up with other Actors and practice scenes together.
15. Take a dance class, especially if interested, in stage performances. Good exercise, balance, and overall health for all.
16. Attend theatre often. Observe carefully and learn. You can try out some small parts, or volunteer to help out on productions behind stage.
17. Go watch movies on the "big screen" to learn and enjoy.
18. Locate websites that offer free acting tips and suggestions. Many sites are available and you can find them by searching.
19. Social media such as Facebook has many actor groups, filmmaking and theatre groups where you can learn about the profession and find jobs.
20. Increase your skills list on your resume by taking classes and learning something new. For example, learn a new language or accent, a new sport, sword fighting, dance, swimming, etc. You never know when a hobby or some obscure skill will be needed.
21. Choose to work out and exercise at home or join a fitness club or group. It is important to maintain your strength, endurance and health.

22. Good grooming habits are important to keep up with so when called for that opportunity you are ready. Examples: a manicure, haircut or styled, necessary makeup on hand, and some nice clothes, which are washed and/or laundered.

23. Consider taking a lesson with a makeup artist in applying makeup. You may decide if you want to choose one for special effects makeup.

CHAPTER ELEVEN

STUDENT FILMS & THE NEXT FIVE YEARS (2002-2006)

Embarking on my journey in the film industry, I found student films to be invaluable. Eager to learn and grow, I set my sights on being cast in a film from the *North Carolina School of the Arts* (NCSA) in Winston Salem, NC. I had heard positive experiences from other Actors who had worked on NCSA projects, and I yearned for a similar experience. The casting process and the project work in student films mirrored those in independent and major Hollywood films, providing a practical learning opportunity for beginners like me. It was a chance to understand the intricacies of the process, from casting to the final product, under the guidance of well-trained film students.

My excitement knew no bounds when I was cast in my first student film, *Get Out of Here* (2000). The film aired several times on the *North Carolina Public Broadcasting Station* (PBS). Although I didn't have a speaking role, I was featured prominently in the "plasticware party scene," a fact that didn't go unnoticed by viewers. This experience underscored the importance of visibility and screen presence in acting, regardless of the size of the role.

In 2001, I continued my journey with another student film, *Birth of a Rebellion*, set in a speakeasy scene. My first speaking role came two years later in a film called *Clay* (2002). Even though my scene was short, the thrill of speaking on film was immense. This experience highlighted the significance of dialogue delivery and voice modulation in acting.

Student films range from about five minutes for freshmen projects to around fifteen or twenty minutes for senior films. They can offer diverse opportunities. One such film was *Haunted Mind*, where I portrayed the mother of a child who had been abused by his father. This role was a stark reminder of the power of cinema to shed light on societal issues like child abuse.

This narrative serves as an educational insight into the world of acting, highlighting the importance of starting small, learning from each experience, and the power of cinema to reflect and address societal issues. Remember, every role, no matter how small, contributes to your growth as an actor and the impact of the film.

Three years had passed since my last student film when, in 2005, I found myself working on two more - *QVC* and *Mr. Bob*. In *QVC*, I landed the lead role, a psychological drama that reason-ated with me due to my background in psychology. My role in *Mr. Bob*, however, was brief. These experiences marked the end of my journey with student films.

I felt ready to move on, to explore new horizons. I began to secure roles in independent films and commercials, building upon the foundation laid by my student film experiences. I would highly recommend this path to other budding Actors. The variety of roles one gets to play in student films not only enriches one's acting reel but also provides invaluable on-set experience.

A professional actor friend of mine continues to work on student films alongside his professional projects, a testament to the value these experiences can add to an actor's career.

Between 2002 and 2005, I worked on several low/no pay independent film projects. These included *Contempt, Brittany's Summer in Paris, Louie the Moon, Cowboy Trail, Cleanup on Aisle Five, Deception, Midnight Ruby* (which was entered into the *Good Morning America* contest in 2004), *All You Can Eat* (a TV series which aired on television in South Carolina), The *Customer is Always Right, Man of Memory, Morning Song Way, Will to Power*, and *Foresight*.

This narrative serves as an educational insight into the world of acting, highlighting the importance of starting small, learning from each experience, and the power of cinema to reflect and address societal issues. Remember, every role, no matter how small, contributes to your growth as an actor and the impact of the film.

In the realm of acting, every role, every line spoken, is a movement toward growth and confidence. Over a span of five years, I transitioned from student films to speaking roles in numerous low-budget independent films. Simultaneously, I found myself cast as an extra in higher budget SAG-AFTRA films such as *Shallow Hal, Stateside, Summer Catch, Loggerhead, Gravedancers,* and *Cold Storage*. My presence also extended to television, where I worked in the background for projects like *Dawson's Creek* and *Surface*.

During this period, another door opened for me – industrial / training films. These films, covering a wide array of topics, offered a unique platform for Actors. My first venture into this domain was in 2002, with an educational company called *Failure Free Reading*. I had the privilege of working with a friend on my first speaking role about 'Interviewing Techniques'. This experience underscored the importance of effective communication and preparation in acting.

Parallel to my acting career, I also ventured into hosting shows for *Eno River Media Productions* and *Across the Canvas Productions*. I found immense joy in co-hosting and hosting these talk shows, which involved interviewing guests. I continued to co-host the local *Live at Nine Show* and occasionally co-host *Blank Surfaces* when there were special shows of interest.

This narrative serves as an educational insight into the world of acting, highlighting the importance of versatility, continuous learning, and seizing every opportunity that comes your way. Remember, every role, no matter how small, contributes to your growth as an actor and the impact of the film.

During this phase of my journey in the acting world, I found myself venturing into new territories. One such adventure was working on a music video for a singer named Courtney Bass in Pawley's Island, South Carolina. This experience, which involved slow dancing with my husband, was a departure from my usual roles. It not only added a new dimension to my skills but also prepared me for future music videos that would bring me significant exposure. This underscores the importance of embracing new opportunities, especially early in one's career, as they can provide invaluable experience and help identify the genre that resonates most with you.

Another novel experience was participating in a touring play, presented on university campuses. While I enjoyed the experience of performing at one university, I realized this particular avenue wasn't quite my *cup of tea*. This experience taught me it's essential to explore different venues and mediums in acting. It helps you understand your preferences and guides you in shaping your career path.

One of the most exciting projects I worked on was for the *History Channel*. I was cast as the head nurse in *Days that Shook the World-Attack on Pearl Harbor* (2004). This role was not just an acting assignment, but a chance to be a part of a project aimed to recreate and commemorating with a significant event in history. More details about this experience can be found in Chapter 14 on documentaries.

This narrative serves as an educational insight into the world of acting, highlighting the importance of exploring diverse roles, learning from each experience, and the significance of historical portrayals in media. Remember, every role, no matter how small, contributes to your growth as an actor and the impact of the film.

During this period of my acting journey, the variety of projects I encountered was both surprising and exhilarating. One such project was *The Sit In at Woolworth* (2004), filmed for the *NAACP Museum* in Greensboro, North Carolina. As a featured extra, I had the opportunity to reenact a significant historical event, providing me with a deeper understanding of the struggles African Americans faced. This experience underscored the educational value of working on historical projects, which can enrich one's knowledge and understanding.

The highlight of this five-year period was landing a role in a national commercial. I played the part of the nosy neighbor in the very first *Travelocity Commercial* featuring the traveling gnome. This experience, which I'll delve into more in the next chapter, emphasized the diverse opportunities available in the acting industry.

As 2005 drew to a close, a pleasant surprise awaited me. A friend, Tasha Holland, revealed an article I had written in 2003 that had been published in *Backstage New York*. I had submitted the article for an online contest that promised to print entries that made them laugh. My entry titled, "A Funny Thing Happened On the Way to My Audition," was the winner, but due to a computer crash, I never received the notification. If it hadn't been for Tasha, I would have remained oblivious to this achievement. This incident highlighted the importance of resilience and the unexpected rewards that can come from perseverance in the acting industry. *Thank you, Tasha Holland!*

The year 2006 unfurled with a flourish, marking my first significant callback for a film titled, *Déjà vu* starring Denzel Washington. A callback, a pivotal moment in an actors' journey, is when you are shortlisted among a handful of Actors for an in-person audition with the Director and other key members of the Casting Team. This experience took me to Atlanta, Georgia, where I auditioned for the renowned Director, Tony Scott. Although I didn't secure the role, the opportunity to audition for such a distinguished Director was exhilarating and educational.

As the year drew to a close, another unique experience awaited me. I was cast in the lead reenactment role in a nationally televised series called *Psychic Detectives*. Filmed in the intriguing locale of Plains, Virginia, this project offered a rich learning experience. Accompanied by my daughter, we stayed in a local B&B, soaking in the local culture and history during my downtime from filming.

An intriguing aspect of our stay was the discovery our B&B was reputed to be haunted. We reveled in the stories about the house's history, adding a layer of intrigue to our experience. More about this can be found in my chapter on re-enactments.

This narrative serves as an educational insight into the world of acting, highlighting the importance of seizing opportunities, learning from each experience, and the significance of immersing oneself in the environment and history of a filming location. Remember, every role, no matter how small, contributes to your growth as an actor and the impact of the film.

THE TAPESTRY OF OPPORTUNITY

A JOURNEY IN ENTERTAINMENT

Once upon a spotlight-drenched time, in the heart of the entertainment industry, I embarked on a quest to unravel the secrets of showbiz, to dance with the limelight, and to whisper my lines to the eager ears of the world. Little did I know this journey would lead me through a kaleidoscope of genres, each more enchanting than the last.

Picture this: the neon glow of Broadway, the hushed intimacy of a recording studio, the sprawling sets of a blockbuster film, and the cozy corner of a voiceover booth. Yes, my friends, the entertainment business is a grand theater with countless stages, and I—like a curious child—explored them all.

Things To Consider

Ah, the voiceover projects! They were my secret garden, where words bloomed into characters, and silence spoke volumes. From animated dragons to sultry perfume ads, my vocal cords danced across scripts like nimble acrobats. I let my voice to heroes, villains, and everything in between. And oh, the thrill of slipping into another skin, of becoming the echo of imagination itself!

The Many Masks of Genre

But let's rewind. Before the voiceovers; before the footlights, there was a revelation: genres. Oh, the myriad flavors of storytelling! Some Actors, they say, specialize—like a master chef perfecting a signature dish. But not I. No, I was a sampler, a wanderer through the buffet of creativity. From rom-coms to sci-fi epics, I tasted them all.

In the sultry heat of the Carolinas, where magnolias whispered secrets, I realized something profound. There wasn't enough work for a single flavor. So, I embraced the smorgasbord. Drama, comedy, mystery—I spun my web across them all. And yes, I became a *Jack Of All Trades. But was I a master of none?* That's the eternal question, my dear budding Actors.

The Cost of Versatility

Now, let's talk about the price of versatility. It's not just applause and bouquets; it is sweat-soaked rehearsals, late nights, and bank accounts gasping for air. Each genre demanded its toll. Training workshops—some as intense as a tempest—shaped me. I learned to pirouette on stage, to modulate my voice like a maestro, and to cry on cue (which, let me tell you, is not as glamorous as it sounds).

And then there were the tools—the sacred artifacts of our trade. An Actor's Toolbox is a treasure chest: headshots, reels, and websites. If you are a singer, add vocal samples to that list. These tools are not mere trinkets; they are the keys to locked doors. Without them, you're a minstrel without a lute.

The Guiding Stars: Focus and Preparation

So, my fledgling stars, here is my counsel: focus. Like a hawk eyeing its prey, choose your top two genres—the ones that set your heart ablaze. Dive deep. Train relentlessly. Become a virtuoso in those realms. Let your acting soul marinate in their essence.

And then, prepare. Gather your tools—the polished sword of your acting reel, the captivating allure of your voice-over samples. Be professional, even when the stage whispers secrets, and the spotlight blinds you. Remember, the world does not applaud half-heartedness.

TESTING THE WATERS, RIDING THE WAVES

But wait! Before you anchor yourself, test the waters. Dip your toes in the sea of genres. Try comedy, feel the rhythm of noir, taste the bittersweet notes of tragedy. *Who knows?* Perhaps you'll discover a hidden cove where your talents bloom like rare orchids. And there, my friends, lies opportunity—the sweetest siren song.

You are the weavers of dreams! Break a leg!

ACTOR TRAINING INSIGHTS & TIDBITS

Key Points to Consider

1. Improvisation (improv) is a very important skill to learn. The Encyclopedia Britannica defines it as: "The playing of dramatic scenes without written dialogue and with minimal or no predetermined dramatic activity." What most often appears to me is adding a bit of your own natural personality and reality to the scene.
2. It can be helpful to participate in an improv acting class. I took one at the beginning of my career. It is a good way to learn how to be more spontaneous in your scenes with your dialogue and actions.
3. Learning improv techniques is also a good tool to use when hosting a talk show. This demonstrates how learning can be transferred from one thing to another. (e.g.: from acting to hosting a talk show)

Smoking my cigar in the saloon on the set of Cowboy Trail.

With Barry McGee and Richard King on the set of Cowboy Trail.

With Gavan Dowdy (my grandson) on location at Circle M City in Sanford, NC. Photo by Lance Britt.

On the set of Cold Storage with Jeffery Pillars.

"Good things take time."
Trade Secrets
by
Releasing 2026
www.donnaink.shop
www.donnaink.net

"Sometimes surprises
can come in nice little packages!"
Trade Secrets
by
Releasing 2026
www.donnaink.shop
www.donnaink.net

CHAPTER TWELVE

MY BIG BREAK: A NATIONAL COMMERCIAL

THE GNOME'S WHIMSICAL WALTZ

In the quiet dawn of 2003, my acting journey tiptoed into existence. A handful of projects graced my path—a couple of Indie films here, a short film there. The stage was set, but the spotlight remained elusive, like a shy star peeking through velvet curtains.

A Tale of Unexpected Stardom

And then, one fateful day, the digital winds whispered secrets. An Internet portal beckoned—an audition call for a web commercial. Raleigh awaited, its streets humming with possibility. But doubts tugged at my sleeve. *Why bother? Why ride those miles for a mere chance?*

Yet, destiny pirouetted in the wings. I, the unsuspecting Actor, saddled up and rode to that audition. The casting room buzzed with anticipation. Lines rehearsed, nerves humming, I stepped into the spotlight. The Casting Director's words hung in the air like a promise: "You're a good actress."

And oh, the call—the sweet symphony of confirmation. I was cast! The thrill surged through me, a champagne bubble of joy. But little did I know this web commercial would unfurl into something grander—a national spectacle, a dance with fame.

The day arrived—the set, the lights, the scripted lines. But between takes, magic happened. My fellow actor and I—like mischievous sprites—played, improvised, and laughed. Unbeknownst to us, the camera drank it all in. Those candid moments, those unscripted whispers—they wove a spell.

And then, the revelation: *our playful banter would grace not just the web but the grand stage of national television*. The gnome—the whimsical wanderer—came alive during the *Rose Bowl* on January 1, 2004. Millions watched; their eyes wide as constellations. But here's the twist: they aired our improvisation lines—the unguarded laughter, the spontaneous spark. Not the rehearsed script, but the magic we spun between takes. The gnome, forever roaming, became my silent accomplice. And *Travelocity's* commercial danced ac-ross screens, leaving a trail of wonder.

Now, dear production company, listen closely. Imagine the gnome returning to his Durham yard—the same cobble-stones where we waltzed with laughter. Imagine me, the actress, waiting in the wings. *Wouldn't that be a delightful en-core-a nod to fate, a wink to the stars?*

So, let this tale ripple through the ether—a reminder that sometimes, the unscripted moments steal the show. And as the gnome roams, I'll whisper to the wind: *Bring him home, let the magic bloom once more.*

Who can tell? Perhaps the gnome might reciprocate with a wink. One of my aspirations was to feature in a nationwide advertisement, and I was pleasantly surprised when this opportunity presented itself earlier than anticipated. The highlight was that it qualified me for membership in the *Screen Actors Guild (SAG)*, a goal I had set since the inception of my career. It's intriguing to think I almost decided against attending the audition that day. What began as a year with limited job prospects ended on a high note! That's the beauty of this industry - the unpredictability. You never know who might be on the other side of the line or what thrilling opportunities or projects might be on the horizon. This commercial, which was broadcast during the *Rose Bowl*, marked the commencement of the *Gnome Campaign*. However, since it was aired only once, there were no residuals or substantial earnings. But hey, wealth isn't everything, and I still had the privilege of featuring in a nationwide commercial.

AUTHOR'S NOTATIONS

A surprise outcome from something that seems ordinary or routine may be fate or it could be skill meeting up with possibility! Maybe my improvisation skills are better than my delivery of scripted dialogue. I guess one can wonder sometimes as to why or how something happens or comes about. No matter the 'how' or 'why,' I was most excited when I was told the commercial was going national. The producers made this decision the very day I worked. Being able to join *SAG-AFTRA* or at least becoming eligible is a goal of many Actors. If we do have this opportunity, it allows us to think that we have reached professionalism in the industry.

ACTOR TRAINING INSIGHTS & TIDBITS

Key Points to Consider

1. If you want to learn more about the *Screen Actors Guild/ American Federation of Television and Radio Artists* (SAG-AFTRA), links to read more are located in Appendix B.

2. If Actors choose not to join the union and join, *Financial Core* (Fi-Core) instead, they are permitted to perform both union and non-union projects while avoiding full SAG membership. Links for *Fi-Core* are featured in Appendix B.

3. A large percentage of Actors remain non-union and are not interested in joining the union. https://www.projectcasting.com/blog/tips-and-advice/union-vs-non-union-acting explains the differences between union and non-union acting and is featured in Appendix B.

4. Appendices A, C, and D provide more Author resources.

"Don't wait for extraordinary opportunities. Seize common occasions and make them great. Weak men wait for opportunities; strong men make them."
Trade Secrets
Releasing 2026
www.donnaink.shop
www.donnaink.net

"Opportunities don't come knocking on the door. They present themselves when you knock the door down!"
Trade Secrets
Releasing 2026
www.donnaink.shop
www.donnaink.net

CHAPTER THIRTEEN

MORE STAND-IN WORK

My initial foray into stand-in work was with the film *Divine Secrets of the Ya-Ya Sisterhood* (2002). It wasn't until six years later that I had another chance to delve into this role. The first experience was so enjoyable, mingling with the stars, I was eager to embark on the next stand-in journey. However, I soon realized this experience would be quite distinct from my first. In this industry, it's important to remember not all opportunities yield the same experiences. Looking back, this particular instance was rather amusing.

Upon learning a star-studded feature film was set to shoot in Greensboro, North Carolina, I reached out to casting to explore potential roles. As it happened, they were in need of a *universal* stand-in who could fill in for various Actors as required. Eager to reprise this role, I was hired to work on the film titled, *The Key Man.* Over the course of a few days, I stood in for several Actors, the first of whom was Hugo Weaving. Now, Hugo Weaving stands at a towering 6'2", while I measure only 5'4." In a frantic rush the day before, I scoured stores for the highest heels I could find to add a few crucial inches to my stature. Despite finding a pair that added about two inches, simple math would tell you I was still too short. But I was undeterred and resolved to make it work. Given that I was standing in for multiple Actors, they decided to give it a shot with me. To be frank, my first day as Hugo Weaving's stand-in was quite chal-

lenging. The towering heels were so uncomfortable I could barely walk, and they were murder on my feet.

To compound the situation, when they called me to stand in an attempt to match his height, I found myself standing on my tiptoes. I can only speculate how much amusement this must have provided the crew members behind my back. I was doing my utmost to meet expectations. By the time night fell, they ceased calling for me and instead opted for a male crew member to stand in. This was relayed to me by another extra, so I spent the remainder of the evening socializing. While filming a scene with the renowned actor Jack Davenport, known for his roles in several *Pirates of the Caribbean* films, he engaged me in conversation in route to the set. To my surprise, Hugo Weaving emerged and initiated a conversation with me. I was taken aback he would converse with a "lowly" stand-in like me!

He was incredibly kind. I was enamored with his Australian accent. We chatted for quite some time until I was informed I could call it a night. As I was leaving, I told Hugo I looked forward to seeing him the following day. However, that never transpired as they didn't call me back for work the next day. I can't say I was surprised, given how ridiculous I must have looked trying to stand in for him. A few days later, casting called me to stand in for Judy Greer. I was relieved, primarily because our heights were similar and I didn't have to endure those torturous high heels. However, I was disappointed I never got the opportunity to bid Hugo Weaving farewell and secure an autograph. Hugo, if you ever come across this book, you owe me an autograph! I know I was advised against asking celebrities for one, but when you've established a rapport, I believe it's acceptable to make such requests.

As it happened, the feature film *The Key Man* (2011) was screened at the *South by Southwest Film Festival* in the USA and had a limited release in a few other countries. I was dis-heartened I never got the chance to watch it. This is a more common occurrence than one might think. The presence of renowned stars in a film doesn't necessarily guarantee its success. I firmly believe the storyline plays a pivotal role in a film's success.

My next stint as a stand-in came three years later. My Agent put my name forward for the role, and I was called in for an interview. Interestingly, a friend of mine was also interviewed for the same role, and we were both selected as stand-ins. I was thrilled at the prospect of working alongside a friend. This star-studded feature film was titled *Main Street*, and it boasted a cast that included Colin Firth, Ellen Burstyn, Patricia Clarkson, Orlando Bloom, Amber Tamblyn, and Andrew McCarthy. The entire project was shot on location in Durham in 2009.

I was afforded the fantastic opportunity to work with Ellen Burstyn for the second time. Having previously been her body double in *Divine Secrets of the Ya-Ya Sisterhood,* I was now her stand-in and body double once again. I was ecstatic about the prospect of working closely with this incredibly talented actress as her sole stand-in throughout the film. Later in the production, I was asked to stand in for Patricia Clarkson for a couple of days when Ellen Burstyn was off set.

The experience of being a stand-in for this film was as thrilling and enjoyable as my initial stand-in role. Similar to the *Ya-Ya* film, I had the chance to interact with numerous celebrities. I was also invited to the wrap party, a relaxed and enjoyable occasion where I could converse with the stars outside of work. My husband joined me at this event and had the opportunity to meet Director John Doyle, Second Assistant Director Andrew Ward, Colin Firth, Amber Tamblyn, among other Actors and actresses. However, some of the stars had already departed and were unable to attend the wrap party.

On the final day of filming, I bid farewell to Ellen Burstyn. We shared a warm hug and expressed our mutual enjoyment of working together. I believe she appreciated having a stand-in of a similar age, which allowed us to connect on a deeper level. We enjoyed brief chats between scenes, and I came to greatly admire her professionalism and talent. She consistently delivered her lines flawlessly and was always on point. She was kind and courteous toward me, although I noticed she didn't interact much with others apart from Director John Doyle. She seemed to be a private individual, something I can certainly relate to. I had expressed a desire to have a photograph taken with her toward the end of filming. She remembered this and asked the photographer to capture our moment together. I also requested him to take some shots with my camera. This thrilled me, as she remembered my request. However, this almost landed me in trouble with one of the Assistant Directors, as I was late returning to the set due to the photo session. As a stand-in, it's crucial to stay close to the filming location to be readily available. After this incident, I ensured not to repeat this mistake. They had dismissed one of the stand-ins during filming, so from then on, I made sure I was always ready when called, even if I was in the company of one of the stars.

Our filming location was a charming, vintage house in Durham. Once a grand residence in its prime, it was situated right in the heart of the city. Before we began filming, the house served as a business premises. The production company rented it and restored it to its former residential glory. As an enthusiast of old homes and antiques, I found immense joy in working there every day. I spent all but one day at this location. The alternate location was a warehouse featured in the film. It was here, towards the end of the film, that Ms. Burstyn requested a photograph with me.

The production company furnished the house with exquisite antiques. We were only permitted to sit on the antique chairs while working, to ensure they were returned in the same condition as they were rented. During our time there, numerous fans, particularly young girls drawn by Orlando Bloom's fame from *Pirates of the Caribbean*, gathered outside the house hoping to catch a glimpse of him. On one occasion, he stepped out to interact with them during a break. One day, Orlando Bloom brought his stunning supermodel girlfriend to the set. It was a delight to see her, even if it was from afar.

One day, Colin Firth's wife and child paid a visit to the set. It was fascinating to hear him switch from speaking Italian with his wife to using a British accent with others and then adopting a Southern accent for his role in the film. As you get to know the Actors, you realize the depth of their intelligence and talent. Most of them didn't achieve stardom or win Academy Awards without possessing significant talent and capability. Many of the Actors I've met are college or graduate school alumni, with some even having attended Ivy League institutions. Two years after this filming, I watched Colin Firth receive an *Academy Award for Best Actor* for his performance in *The King's Speech.*

As of now, my last stint as a stand-in was for this film. Although I'm currently vying for more prominent roles in feature films and TV, I wouldn't rule out the possibility of doing stand-in work again, as it's quite enjoyable. I find most aspects of this industry appealing, so I don't limit myself strictly to speaking roles. At the end of this chapter, I've included some useful tips for stand-in work. It's worth noting it is easier to get fired for underperforming as a stand-in than as an extra or background Actor, though I've seen both happen. This is a business, and it's crucial to always bear that in mind.

AUTHOR'S NOTATIONS

The second time around for stand-in work was easier, as I knew more about what to expect. Although each experience can be different, you can feel more confident having done it before. Stand-in work pays more than extra work and you are in closer contact with the stars. It provides a good training opportunity as you can observe up close their performance.

HELPFUL TIPS

Stand-In Work Performances

1. *Are you aware that your role involves observing the Star's movements so you can replicate them in the scene?*

   The Star will first rehearse the scene while you watch, and then you'll stand in and mimic their actions while the lighting is adjusted. The Director of Photography (DOP) or Cameraman will ask you to repeat the movements.

2. *Do you understand that you need to be on set and close by so you can observe the actor and be readily available when called?*

   They don't appreciate having to send someone to find you. You'll learn when you can take a break, usually when the actor you're standing in for isn't working on set. However, you must keep an eye out for when the actor returns to set.

3. *Are you aware you shouldn't initiate a conversation with the Star unless they show an interest in talking with you?*

   They are focused on memorizing their lines and their role, so engaging them in conversation could distract them.

4. *Did you know the wardrobe department will provide you with a shirt or outfit similar in color to what the Star will be wearing at the start of each day?*

5. *Are you aware that stand-ins are typically matched to the star based on height, size, hair color, and sometimes skin tone and age range?*

   You may be interviewed or asked to attend a 'go see' before they hire you.

6. *Do you understand the importance of being available when needed?*

   It's advisable to seek permission from the second Assis-tant Director, or whoever is in charge of you, before taking a break.

The Main Street Wrap Party with my husband Danny Sewell.

*The Main Street Wrap Party with Jim Babel,
Danny Sewell, and Colin Firth.*

Main Street set with Colin Firth.

Main Street set with Ellen Burstyn. It's a wrap!

Catherine Sewell on the set of Main Street in 2009.

Catherine Sewell on the set of Main Street in 2009.

Catherine Sewell on the set of Main Street in 2009.

Catherine Sewell on the set of Main Street in 2009.

My stand in performance remains a wonderful memory.
Credit: Creative Commons / Publically Traded.

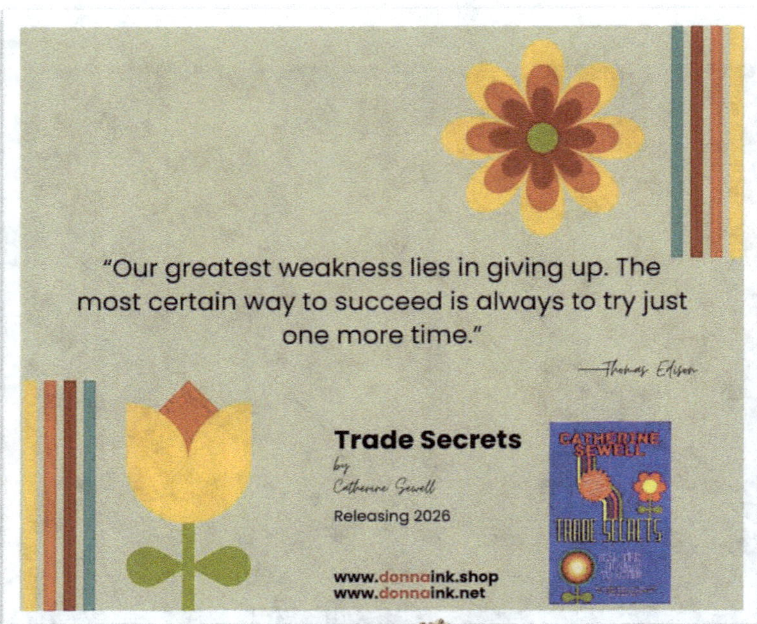
"Our greatest weakness lies in giving up. The most certain way to succeed is always to try just one more time."
—Thomas Edison
Trade Secrets
by
Catherine Sewell
Releasing 2026
www.donnaink.shop
www.donnaink.net
CATHERINE SEWELL
TRADE SECRETS

"The Ultimate form of preparation is not planning for a specific scenario, but a mindset that can handle uncertainty."
— James Clear
Trade Secrets
by
Catherine Sewell
Releasing 2026
www.donnaink.shop
www.donnaink.net
CATHERINE SEWELL
TRADE SECRETS

CHAPTER FOURTEEN

DOCUMENTARY REENACTMENTS/DOCUDRAMA

Documentary reenactments breathe life into the pages of history, recreating events and periods from the past with vivid detail. These shows have carved a niche for themselves on television, with crime reenactments and docu-dramas being particularly popular. These productions often feature a narrator or Subject Matter Experts (SMEs), family members, or other individuals who weave the narrative while Actors bring the past to life through their performances. Interestingly, these reenactment scenes often involve minimal dialogue from the Actors, with the story primarily being told by one or more narrators.

A subset of these shows, known as docudramas, strives to stay true to historical facts while allowing some creative liberty in the finer details. These productions often include dialogue, sometimes even incorporating the actual words spoken by real-life individuals, as documented in historical records. In some instances, producers choose to film these recon-structed events at the actual locations where they originally occurred, adding another layer of authenticity to the production.

My initial venture into the realm of historical document-tary docudramas began with *Days that Shook the World-At-tack on Pearl Harbor* (2004). I took on the role of the Chief Nurse who received the harrowing call about the Japanese bombing of Pearl Harbor. The scene was set with the nurses immersed in casual morning conversation over breakfast, with me still donning hair rollers when the call arrived. This project, shot in Wilmington, had me employed as a day player, a position where an actor is contracted on a daily basis. Despite the brief one-day engagement, the experience was thoroughly rewarding. This project was a production of the *British Broadcasting Corporation* (BBC), and my Director was a Brit with a strong accent. This presented an intriguing and challenging contrast with my pronounced Southern accent.

On one occasion, the Director spontaneously gave me some lines that weren't in the script. I had difficulty understanding him. I nearly echoed what I thought he said, but luckily, I hesitated. If I hadn't, it would have been quite embarrassing as my interpretation was far from what he actually said. I asked him to repeat for clarity. It's always best to seek clarification when in doubt. I narrowly avoided a significant blunder, as what I thought he said could have been offensive to him.

My next venture was a reenactment for the TV series *Psychic Detectives* in 2006. After a two-year gap, I was thrilled to work on another project. The filming took place in the picturesque Plains, Virginia. I assumed the role of Patricia McCormick. Staying at the historic B&B was as enjoyable as the filming itself. I had the opportunity to explore the area, which was delightful. My daughter accompanied me on this trip, making it even more special. I was also cast in another television crime drama called *North Carolina Wanted; Who Killed Linda Meeker?* (2008). I played the role of a grieving mother. I remember feeling elated when the Director / Cinematographer complimented my acting. This was very encouraging, as compliments are rare in this industry. Unfortunately, the North Carolina show only ran for a few short years, and I was saddened to see it end.

Sid Roth's, *It's Supernatural,* a widely watched Christian show, airs weekly. Sid Roth established the *Its Supernatural Network* over twenty years ago with the aim of spreading the knowledge of Jesus to all people. According to Sid Roth, his strategy is to reach out, 'to the Jew first' (Romans 1:16). On the show, he interviews guests who share miracles and healings.

My debut on this show was during the, *Billy Burke Episode* in June 2010, where I portrayed a blind woman who experienced healing. This opportunity was particularly special to me, as I was already a fan of the show. This marked the beginning of a nine-year association with this series. Since 2010, I've collaborated with the show's Director and Casting Director on numerous episodes and projects. Building strong professional relationships is crucial in this industry.

The aim of an Actor is to cultivate these relationships to secure recurring work opportunities. Once you've established this rapport, they become familiar with your work ethic and you gain insight into their expectations. All the episodes I've appeared in are listed on the *International Media Database* (IMDb). As there are several individuals named Catherine Sewell, my name is listed with the Roman numeral I. The last episode I filmed was the *Dave Hayes Episode*, which aired on May 21, 2018.

In this episode, I played a woman suffering from circulatory and other health issues who experienced healing. All the episodes can be viewed at www.SidRoth.org. Two more reenactment shows I have been on were, *Inspiration Today* (*Heaven Series* with Trudy Harris) and *Happily Never After*. The *Heaven Series* was filmed in Charlotte at the Duke Mansion. I played the role of Billie Patterson. That was special to be able to film there and get to see the mansion. It aired on *INSP Network*. *The Happily Never After* Episode: *On the Market for Murder* was filmed in Virginia. I had a lead role as Lou Patten. Unfortunately, the series only aired for two years (2012-2014).

Now, I would like to tell you about the most special of all documentaries; it is the one Tim Marsh and I created, wrote, produced, and edited called, *The House in the Horseshoe. The Alston House* is another name that is used in addition to the *House in the Horseshoe*. It is a historic home built circa 1772 and the site of a *1781 Revolutionary War* skirmish. The house was also the home of four-time North Carolina Governor Benjamin Williams.

Annually, the house becomes a stage for a reenactment of the historical skirmish, with numerous vendors showcasing crafts from that era. Tim and I undertook the task of filming a documentary to recreate the events of that day and period.

The narrative of the story was largely conveyed by the house's Tour Guide and Manager. I had the opportunity to interview a descendant of Colonel Fanning, a Tory who launched an attack on the home while Whig Colonel Alston and his family were present. In 2006, the *North Carolina Society of Historians* honored Tim and I with the *Paul Greene Multimedia Award* for this documentary. We were both thrilled to receive this recognition, particularly as it was our inaugural documentary.

One key takeaway from this project was my realization *I find it much more comfortable to be in front of the camera than behind it!* In essence, I discovered that filmmaking involves a multitude of challenging aspects. I found being an actress aligns better with my skills and interests. However, Tim and I did win the *Paul Greene Multimedia Award* by the *NC Society of Historians,* so I guess I did something right with this documentary project. I do hold immense respect and admiration for the hard work and dedication required to create and produce a film or video project having experienced it myself.

AUTHOR'S NOTATIONS

Documentary film is a favorite of mine as they are non-fictional and often based on historical accounts to document events, people, and places for instruction, information, or education. It is a great way to preserve a historical record. Personally, I had rather read, listen to, and view something derived from actual life experiences - non-fiction opposed to fiction. There is always a lesson to be learned.

ACTOR TRAINING INSIGHTS & TIDBITS

Key Points To Consider

1. If you are interested in acting in documentaries/docu-dramas, perform a search for production companies who produce this genre, such as popular crime shows.
2. There are many crime shows on TV so you can perform an Internet search for the names of the show and the production company. Many times, there will be a casting link on the site where you can find submittal information.
3. You can also find some of these productions or casting companies on Facebook. *Jupiter Casting* is an example of a casting department I have worked with. It is the in-house casting for *Juniper Entertainment*. They cast documentaries / docudramas. I have worked with this company and found them very professional. They are based in Knoxville, Tennessee.

DVD Cover for the House in the Horseshoe video. Winner of the Paul Greene Multimedia Award by the NC Society of Historians.

Nurse in Days That Shook the World: Attack on Pearl Harbor.

"Take note and learn from yours and other's
experiences and apply them as life lessons."
Trade Secrets
Releasing 2026
www.donnaink.shop
www.donnaink.net

"Do unto others as you would
have them do unto you"
Trade Secrets
Releasing 2026
www.donnaink.shop
www.donnaink.net

CHAPTER FIFTEEN

THE NEXT FIVE YEARS (2007-2011)

The year 2007 marked the ongoing journey of the live talk show, *Live at Nine*. I continued to contribute to this show every other Thursday for most months, and occasionally on a fifth Thursday. The show served as a platform for my growth, learning, and confidence-building.

Acclimating to the television environment, particularly live broadcasts, is crucial. Live shows, which are becoming increasingly rare, offer invaluable learning experiences as they demand accuracy on the first attempt. This has been beneficial in my other television and film work, reducing the need for multiple takes.

As 2007 progressed, I found myself involved in more film and television projects. During the summer, I worked on a small independent film titled, *Marshalls, I.T.,* a cowboy-themed movie. The majority of the filming took place in Virginia, with the final days shot at *Circle M City* (also known as *Cowboy Town*) in Sanford, North Carolina. This cowboy town set is an ideal location for filmmakers aiming to create a western film. One notable location in Virginia where I filmed was the *Historic 1908 Courthouse in Independence.*

Every job, regardless of whether the project makes it to the big screen or television, offers valuable lessons and experiences to take away.

Another independent film I had the pleasure of participating in was *Praise Band* (2008). My role was a comedic one,

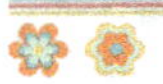

where I auditioned for the church choir with a voice so dreadful I wasn't permitted to finish the song. A highlight of this film was meeting George Hamilton IV, an accomplished and talented musician. He was a singer, guitarist, and songwriter who had forty songs on *Billboard's Country Music Charts* in the 1960s and 1970s. In later years, I had the unique opportunity to visit his childhood home in North Carolina. The house was on the market, and my husband and I, who were house hunting at the time, had the chance to view it. I have a cherished photograph of George Hamilton IV and me on set. Regrettably, he passed away on September 17, 2014.

Recently, a friend called me, brimming with excitement, to tell me she had just spotted me on television. She was casually watching a movie and didn't expect to see me. The movie she was watching was none other than *Praise Band*. I was taken aback as it has been ten years since I filmed that movie. You never know where your work will surface. Unless my friends inform me when they see me, I'm not always aware of when my projects are being broadcast. I usually know the initial airing date of a film or television show, but not subsequent ones. Some television shows, like crime dramas, are broadcast multiple times over a long period.

During the autumn season, I was involved in a television project titled, *Mysteries and Legends of SC* The filming took place in Georgetown, SC, a location that added an element of fun to the experience. I had the privilege of meeting Elizabeth R. Huntsinger, a historian and author known for her book, *The Ghosts of Georgetown*. She also served as a historian spokesperson on the *Weather Channel* for the *Grey Man Ghost of Pawley's Island* episode, which still occasionally airs. Regrettably, due to the producer's illness, the television project Ms. Huntsinger and I collaborated on was left incomplete.

The pinnacle of 2008 was when I had the opportunity to host the Red Carpet for the *WiFi, Gilded Nights Gala* in Wilmington, North Carolina. This event marked the *Screen Actors Guild's Seventy-Fifth Anniversary Celebration*, paying tribute to actor Pat Hingle. This was an entirely new and enjoyable experience for me, as it allowed me to meet numerous renowned and celebrated Actors. The task was challenging, as it required me to familiarize myself with the names of the Actors walking the

Red Carpet and some details about them. I was particularly thrilled to meet Pat Hingle, best known for his role as *Commissioner James Gordon* in the *Batman* series. During our interview, Mr. Hingle was incredibly kind and gracious. Instead of discussing his own achievements, he showed interest in my career, demonstrating his caring nature in addition to his acting prowess. I also attended an acting workshop in Wilmington, NC, where he spoke. His main message to us was to persist, and persevere, in the profession, and *stay in the water*, which has resonated with me and proven to be sound advice.

During this period, I was involved in four independent films: *Goodbye Solo* (2008), *Half Empty* (2009), *Wesley* (2009), and *Teenaged* (2008). Additionally, I continued my work on the talk show *Live at Nine*, hosted another television show titled, *Blank Surfaces*, and appeared in a political commercial for Ric Marshall's campaign for the NC House in Surry County.

The years 2009-2011 were marked by notable projects, such as the film *Main Street*, the *Rusty Bucket Kids Show*, where I played the role of a storekeeper, and *Treme*, a television series filmed in New Orleans. The *Rusty Bucket Kids Show* was a project produced by my friends, J.D. Demers and his wife, Michelle. I thoroughly enjoyed working with them on this television show, the pilot of which aired on the local *TV Station WRAL in Raleigh*. In the television series *Treme*, I shared a scene with John Goodman. Although I didn't watch that episode, I later learned from my Agent I was featured in it.

I also appeared in two more episodes of Sid Roth's, *It's Supernatural*, a promo for *Project 77*, and a music video. Subsequent projects included a principal part in an industrial for *Thera Slim*, an extra role in *The Shunning* which was a television special for *Hallmark*, and a speaking part in another television series called, *Southern Fried Stings*.

One project I am particularly proud of is a music video by Madonna Nash titled, *Dirty Little Secrets*. I took on the com-edic role of a skating rink boss while Madonna performed her song. The scene was set in the 1960s, and I sported a beehive hairdo, which made for a humorous sight. Restoring my hair to its normal state after all that teasing was quite a task!

The video was broadcast on *Country Music Television* (CMT), and I was thrilled to be part of it and to see it air on CMT.

This was a novel experience for me, as I had never before played a lead role in a music video. I was fond of the song, which made it easier to listen to it on repeat during filming. Interestingly, the filming took place at a skating rink. Some of the Actors were expected to be able to skate, but as you might guess, not all of them could. One Actor, who was hired for a featured role, struggled to skate despite his past experience. During one scene where I was being pushed in a wheeled chair at high speed, the chair tipped over, and I ended up on the floor, still strapped to the chair. I wasn't injured, and the incident added a touch of humor to the scene. They even used that shot in the video. You can watch the video on YouTube.

Another unique experience was filming a book video promo for *The Gathering Storm*. This was a first for me, as I had never heard of book videos before this. I'm not sure how it turned out for the author, but I found the concept intriguing.

Lastly, I had a speaking role in a *SAG-AFTRA* short film titled *Tobaccoland: Before* (2012), which was filmed in North Carolina.

AUTHOR'S NOTATIONS

This chapter could almost be called, *Variety in the entertainment business is the spice of life.* The quote "Variety is the very spice of life, that gives it all its flavor," is from William Cowper's poem, *The Task*. This chapter has a variety of experiences and some completely new for me. This is like the flavoring in cake—a delightful taste of new opportunities.

ACTOR TRAINING INSIGHTS & TIDBITS

Key Points To Consider

1. Don't be afraid to search out and try new things. We learn more about ourselves and capabilities when we experience a variety of things.
2. Having a strong professional network is so important. By networking and meeting people in this business, you are able to learn about job opportunities. Consider meeting diverse industry people in addition to fellow Actors.
3. Marketing yourself is another important way to expand your possibilities. It goes without saying you are well-advised to create a website, maintain a blog, participate in social media, etc. Also, create a social marketing campaign. Define your Type and Brand. Create your own project to showcase your talent.

The Rusty Bucket Kids Show Premier with Jerry Mathers.

The Rusty Bucket Kids Show Premier with Jerry Mathers.

With George Hamilton IV in Praise Band,
The Rusty Bucket Kids Show Premier with Charlie Gaddy.

With Jim Dilettoso, Deidre Dowdy, and Robert Harris
at a Carolina Actors Action Network party.

Dirty Little Secrets Music Video with Madonna Nash.

Help! I'm falling!

The RUSTY BUCKET
KIDS.COM
RBKC, INC. PRESENTS "THE RUSTY BUCKET KIDS"
INTRODUCING BY SPECIAL APPEARANCE CHARLIE GADDY AS "GRANDPA PEAKSSEN"
INTRODUCING ROXANNA DEMERS JOHNCOLEMAN DEMERS SCOTT ANDREW TAYLOR AKIN WILLIAMS PABLO VEGA
WITH MARK ROBERTS CLAUDIO OSWALD NIEDWOROK IRENE SANTIAGO J.C. KNOWLES
COMPOSER CRAIG BRANDWYNNE SONGS PERFORMED BY G.W. PIERCE & THE RUSTY BUCKET BAND
DIRECTOR OF PHOTOGRAPHY FLIP MINOTT ART DIRECTOR DENISE SCHUMAKER EDITED BY COLE RUSSING AND IAN KRABACHER
PRODUCED BY SIMON BARRON JOHN M. DEMERS AND KEVIN ROBERT MCDERMOTT
EXECUTIVE PRODUCERS JOHN M. DEMERS AND MICHELLE HOWE DEMERS
STORY BY JOHN M. DEMERS WRITTEN AND DIRECTED BY KEVIN ROBERT MCDERMOTT
golden corral
WWW.THERUSTYBUCKETKIDS.COM
SOUNDTRACK AVAILABLE ON

"Variety is the very spice of life,
that gives it all its flavor.."
Trade Secrets
by
www.donnaink.shop
www.donnaink.net

"Imagination is everything.
It is the preview of life's coming attractions."
Trade Secrets
by
www.donnaink.shop
www.donnaink.net

CHAPTER SIXTEEN

INDUSTRIALS/TRAINING FILMS: A NEW EXPERIENCE

Industrials, also known as training films, are tailored by industries to fulfill specific needs. A case in point is an industrial I participated in, which showcased interviewing techniques for a company named, *Failure Free Reading*. This marked my debut in training films. I recall feeling quite nervous about the experience, particularly about remembering my lines. Regrettably, a seldom-occurring nervous tic (a head movement) surfaced that day while I was filming the scene. I noticed this issue and attempted to relax to prevent it from showing up. Later, a fellow actor informed me the tic was visible on screen. The producer and editor likely faced challenges trying to edit around it. I felt remorseful for causing them this inconvenience. However, such incidents can occur when you're starting out with new and diverse projects and grappling with nerves and uncertainty about your skills.

This was early in my career. I strived to learn from it and move forward. Interestingly, I've never experienced the tic again since then. I feared it could jeopardize my career if it persisted, especially since my father developed a similar tic later in his life. It astonishes me even when I'm nervous, it doesn't resurface.

In the same year, I had the chance to work on another training film for the *Alzheimer's Association*. I was hired as an extra, so I didn't have the stress of memorizing lines like in my first industrial. As it turned out, I did end up delivering a line or two that aligned with the script. This was my first opportunity to employ an acting skill known as improvisation. This technique, often used by Actors to add lines that complement the storyline and extend beyond the written script, is frequently encouraged by film or project Directors.

I've come across projects that are entirely based on improvisation. One activity that unexpectedly honed this skill for me was creating numerous stories for my young daughter. I had no inkling this would serve as preparation for a crucial acting skill. I also attended an improvisation workshop, which I found to be a beneficial resource for enhancing this skill.

It's intriguing how opportunities in a specific area can cluster within the same year. I was engaged to work on another training film for a prominent university in North Carolina. With a substantial script to memorize, I was apprehensive about this project. As I began the first scene, I felt things were progressing well until the Director abruptly halted me. He then began auditioning other Actors to replace me, leaving everyone, including me, stunned. He didn't explain his dissatisfaction and continued to audition extras for my role. Eventually, he selected a male actor to replace me, and I was relegated to an extra. I sought feedback from two other extras who had a clear view of my performance, asking them what I had done wrong. They assured me they didn't see any mistakes and thought I was doing a good job. I did notice the Director smelled of alcohol and may have been drinking before coming to set. I also wondered if gender and race played a role in his decision to replace me with a male. This experience was hurtful and embarrassing, but my background as a psychologist helped me understand the Director likely had his own issues.

I share this anecdote to highlight Actors, like professionals in any field, encounter various challenges and difficulties in their careers. The world of acting can be demanding in numerous ways. Despite reassurances from my fellow extras about the quality of my work, I found myself questioning whether I should quit. The experience was so distressing I wept all the way home and couldn't bring myself to share it with my husband out of sheer embarrassment. To this day, I'm unsure what the Director disliked in my performance as he didn't provide any feedback when I asked. This was an unprecedented and isolated incident in my career. The key takeaway from this experience is unexpected things happen sometimes; the rea-sons for them may remain unknown. The important thing is to pick yourself up and keep moving forward, which is exactly what I did.

Interestingly, 2002 was the year when I participated in the most industrials to date within a single year. These industrials also had the most dialogue, except for one medical industrial. The challenge was I was still in the early stages of my career and lacked confidence. However, the only way to gain confidence is to dive in, gain experience, and learn from it. Industrials are my least preferred projects in this business. They often involve extensive scripts, sometimes spanning several pages, which the lead actor must memorize. The scripts can contain highly technical language that can be difficult to pronounce, especially medical terms. I encountered this in an industrial I worked on years later, where I had to seek help from a doctor friend to pronounce certain medications.

At times, you may be lucky enough to have a teleprompter displaying your lines; however, using one requires specific training. This industry necessitates specialized training for all areas you may wish to explore. Industrials sometimes demand a more professional appearance for casting. My look is more aligned with film and television, which I find more enjoyable. Nevertheless, when an audition call comes, I seize the opportunity as they often pay well, and some can be more enjoyable than others. Some Actors prefer to specialize or concentrate on industrials and can secure a lot of work in this area. I've ventured into all facets of entertainment business. Since my initial year of industrial/training films, I've continued to participate in one or two each year. Every experience serves as preparation for future projects and boosts your confidence. And yes, we older folks can indeed learn new tricks. I've found that my memory has significantly improved since I embarked on this career, thanks to constant practice.

Despite common beliefs memory declines with age, I can attest, mine has improved. I must mention I had a good memory during my school years. Memorizing Bible verses in elementary school and quotations in middle school enhanced my memory skills. In middle school, my science teacher offered extra credit for every quotation we memorized and wrote at the end of our tests. I always had extra points added to my grade. He introduced his students to John Bartlett's quotations, which I've enjoyed reading and quoting ever since. This is why I liked to quote them at the end of *Live at Nine*, as I mentioned in an earlier chapter. The old saying "use it or lose it" may apply here when it comes to memory. If you're considering a career in this industry, stay positive, determined, and go for it. Persistence does pay off; however, be prepared to undergo training and to work hard.

AUTHOR ANNOTATIONS & GOOD TO KNOWS

New experiences can bring challenges to face and learn from. My very first training film I had to deal with and confront my physical issue. In another was my reckoning with rejection. Maybe because of these two experiences, especially the last, I have become stronger and more determined to deal with the many rejections an actor faces in their career. Generally, Actors audition for roles many more times than we book. There are many factors that are involved in the selection process. We need to understand this and not let rejection impede our trying.

ACTOR TRAINING INSIGHTS & TIDBITS

Key Points To Consider

1. *What are industrial films?*

   According to John Casablancas www.jcasablancas.com/what-are-industrial-films 11-26-12. *Industrials are corporate films, made by businesses for use in training or motivating employees!*

   There is on-camera work for talent and narration work for voice talent too! Industrial films typically have lots of corporate terminology – words Actors aren't expected to personally know what they mean but have the job of mak-ing it seem they understand every word spoken!

2. Voice talent training is another skill area that can provide additional work opportunities for the trained and skilled actor. I discussed in an earlier chapter my struggles with my

Southern accent. A neutral accent is what is most commonly used for voice talent work.

3. Memory techniques can be helpful for Actors to learn their lines:

    a) Read your lines carefully and try to understand thoroughly what you are saying. If you don't completely understand what you are saying and why, then it will be more difficult to remember.

    b) Write your lines out by hand. Some people are visual learners and benefit from this technique.

    c) Run your lines with someone else.

    d) Memorize one line at a time.

    e) Learn your cue lines. (These are the lines read by the other actor that precedes your lines).

    f) Visualize your script lines.

    g) Move around and/or do things while saying your lines.

    h) Repetition, repetition, repetition.

Catherine filming for a medical industrial.

Catherine and Danny Sewell.

"Develop a passion for learning. If you do, you will never cease to grow."
—Anthony J D'Angelo
Trade Secrets
by
Catherine Sewell
Releasing 2026
www.donnaink.shop
www.donnaink.net
CATHERINE SEWELL
TRADE SECRETS

"Most men lead lives of quiet desperation and go to the grave with the song still in them!"
—David Thoreau
Trade Secrets
by
Catherine Sewell
Releasing 2026
www.donnaink.shop
www.donnaink.net
CATHERINE SEWELL
TRADE SECRETS

CHAPTER SEVENTEEN

HIGHLIGHTS FROM 2012 TO 2016

The commencement of this five-year journey was characterized by extensive travel. I had an audition in New Orleans for an industrial, followed by another audition in Richmond, Virginia, two weeks later. In the early stages of my career and during parts of this five-year period, live auditions were the norm. Regardless of the distance, even if it was several hundred miles away, travel was necessary if you were keen on securing the job. Fortunately, I had the opportunity to audition closer to home in North Carolina. The current trend leans toward remote auditions.

As an actor, you're responsible for recording your audition, either using your own equipment or hiring someone to do it. The recording is then sent to your Agent or Casting Di-rector via email or uploaded to a specific website like Actors' Access. I appreciate that the initial auditioning process is now predominantly remote, as it saves considerable time and money. Investing upfront in a good video camera, filming equipment, and a computer with editing and conversion soft-ware is worthwhile, as it results in overall time and cost savings. Some Actors even use their cell phones for this purpose. One advantage of remote auditioning is the reduced stress compared to a live audition. I find it more relaxing to have my husband film me. However, if you receive a callback, you'll usually have to attend the audition in person. Occasionally, you can use Skype, Zoom, or another remote platform for call-backs. As I mentioned earlier, a callback is a second audition invitation extended to a smaller group of Actors. The list of Actors is narrowed down to the top choices. Sometimes, you might be cast directly from the remote video audition you or your Agent sent to the Casting Director. I find it gratifying when this happens, and it does occur quite frequently.

For your information, neither of the auditions required extensive travel resulted in a booking. That's just the nature of the game in this industry. One thing you must come to terms with is rejection. It is essential to develop resilience, not take it personally, and simply move on to the next opportunity. If you are serious about this business and invest in proper training, there's always another audition around the corner. When I first started, auditions were few and far between, and landing jobs was even rarer. You need to cultivate your unique style and hone your acting skills. Watching Actors perform may seem effortless, but that's because they are highly skilled. It requires learning and practice to make your acting appear natural rather than forced.

In 2012, I worked on several projects, including *Divorce Care* with a *Church Initiative* based in Wake Forest, an *INSP Network* show called *Heaven Series,* where I played the role of Billie Patterson, an independent television pilot called, *The Observer,* and a soap opera titled, *Cool Carolina Nights*. Unfortunately, one of the producers of *The Observer* passed away after we had done a significant amount of filming in 2012 and 2013, and filming has not resumed since.

A thrilling film opportunity arose in 2013, when I was cast in the SAG feature film *Elbow Grease,* now retitled *An Innocent Kiss.* This was particularly special because I had the chance to work with Burt Reynolds. I played the role of Granny Blythe, the mother of the lead character Ellie Barnes, portrayed by Whitney Goin. My part of the movie was filmed in the small community of Townville in upstate South Carolina, near the Town of Seneca. It was delightful to be in that part of the state again as I have family there. Working with Burt Reynolds was a joy as he was very friendly and kind. He was open to taking pictures with us. Having watched him for many years in films such as the *Smokey and the Bandit* series, I never could have imagined I would one day work alongside Mr. Reynolds in a movie.

That year, I was part of the background cast in the feature film *Tammy,* starring Melissa McCarthy, Susan Sarandon, and Kathy Bates. The filming took place in Wilmington. I was on set for two days. The scene was set outdoors, depicting a market with vendors in a park. A good friend accompanied me on the first day, and we had the chance to see Susan Sarandon and Melissa McCarthy. She decided not to return for the second day, finding the experience enough for her. The weather was hot, and the food on set left much to be desired. Back-groundwork isn't for everyone. I'm accustomed to the varying conditions of different sets and the long, challenging days, but I always manage to learn something.

I was presented with a wonderful opportunity to work on a short film titled *Junebug,* where I embodied the character of Aunt Mable, the great aunt of a young girl named Junebug. The film was inspired by a summer from the Writer / Director's own life. This experience was invaluable to me as it involved memorizing an extensive script, which subsequently proved beneficial for my future projects. The majority of the film was shot in a residence in Fuquay Varina, NC. A screening of the film was conducted in Cary at a theater, where time was set aside for feedback on this and other showcased films. *Junebug* received positive reviews, and the audience suggested it be expanded into a full-feature film. This was a pivotal moment for me as I received constructive feedback on my role from individuals who were unaware of my presence at the time. Every experience serves as a learning moment if we learn and grow from it.

In 2015, I was presented with two *SAG-AFTRA* film opportunities: *A Lovely Sunrise* (2016) and *Fever Dreams: It's My House*. In *A Lovely Sunrise,* I played a supporting role as Mandy. The filming took place in Clayton, NC, which was a manageable commute for me. *Fever Dreams: It's My House* is a suspenseful horror film composed of several vignettes. In my vignette, Keith Harris, Owen Daly, and I were the lead characters. The conclusion of the vignette was quite surprising and thrilling. I thoroughly enjoyed watching the film and attending the wrap party afterward. *The* movie *Fever Dreams* has won several awards.

In the fall of 2015, I had the opportunity to work as an extra on the film *Imperium* (2016) in Hopewell, Virginia. The film starred Daniel Radcliffe, Toni Collette, and Tracy Letts. I played the role of a restaurant patron in the scene I worked on. During a break in filming, one of the other extras and I were sitting in a booth at the restaurant when Daniel Radcliffe walked past our booth and stopped to chat with us. We conversed for a few minutes. He was very kind. He even autographed something for me to give to my daughter. His role in this movie was a significant departure from his roles in the Harry Potter series. It was intriguing to see him as an adult, given he was quite young when he starred in the Harry Potter series. This experience and meeting Daniel Radcliffe were truly enjoyable.

The summer of 2016 was filled with excitement as I received a call back in Atlanta for a significant television show. This boosted my confidence, affirming my acting skills were improving and enabling me to compete with the stiff competition for these roles. Regardless of the size of the role or the number of lines, the competition is fierce. Many people have expressed they would be content with just one line, assuming it wouldn't be too challenging. However, even the most accomplished Actors may not secure even a one-line role. Numerous factors influence whether you land a role, and they're not solely based on your acting skills. All conditions must align perfectly. For instance, if you bear a resemblance to the producer's disliked mother-in-law, you may not get the job. I was once a finalist for a role, only to learn the Director had hired his mother. On another occasion, a similar situation occurred, but the Director/Producer hired his girlfriend's mother. I didn't feel as defeated as I knew talent wasn't the deciding factor!

A unique opportunity presented itself in 2016 through the media company, *Across the Canvas Productions*. I was hired to attend the *Thirty-fifth Spring Water Festival* in Williamston, South Carolina, to interview some of the celebrities and bands performing there. It was thrilling to meet and interview T.G. Sheppard, who delivered an outstanding performance at the festival. He is recognized as a Classic Country Artist. Other musicians I interviewed included Shelby Raye of the *Shelby Raye Band*, a talented young teenage artist who sings country, and the *Odyssey Band*, who play old school and R&B music. Their performance was fantastic, and I thoroughly enjoyed it as R&B is one of my favorite music genres. Some of the interviews were broadcast on *Blank Surfaces*, but unfortunately, due to technical issues with the filming, T.G. Sheppard's interview wasn't aired.

Another memorable moment of the year was finally geting the chance to meet my Agents from Louisiana, Dawn and George Landrum of *Landrum Arts Louisiana*. They were invited to judge a competition in Atlanta and decided to host a Christmas gathering at a hotel to meet their Atlanta-based Actors and anyone else willing to travel. Having been with them for seventeen years, I felt it was high time to meet them in person. My husband Danny joined me, and we had a wonderful time meeting them and the local Atlanta Actors. They run a family agency and are incredibly talented, professional Agents, and genuinely wonderful people. It's not uncommon for talent to go years without meeting their Agents if they're based in different states. My acceptance into the agency was based on my headshot, resume, and work reel submissions.

I started with them at the very beginning, so to speak, when they were just starting out. Now, they're well-known and respected nationwide. For tips on finding an Agent, refer to my suggestions at the end of this chapter and in the Extro.

AUTHOR ANNOTATIONS & GOOD TO KNOWS

Since the beginning of my career in the entertainment business, there have been quite a few changes. The main change has been in the area of technology. In person *live* auditions are now mostly done through self-tapings and call back is a Skype, Zoom, or other platform session with casting and the production company. It just depends on the production company as to whether they want to have a callback in person or not.

Since self-taping for auditions is the norm now, it is important to invest in good equipment if you prefer to tape with a video camera. Many Actors now use their cellphone to tape an audition. Since I have all the taping equipment necessary to tape my audition, I prefer using it and not taping on my cellular. However, as I found out, it is a good idea to learn how to tape and edit on your cell in case you are away from home traveling.

Actor Training Insights And Tidbits

Key Points To Consider

Tips On Finding And Signing With A Talent Agent

1. Ensure you possess relevant skills and experience to present to the agency before expecting them to represent you.
2. Compile a list of your unique talents and abilities that could be beneficial in the entertainment industry. For instance, vocal abilities, dancing, acting training, previous theatre experience, or vocal skills.
3. Create an additional list of special skills you possess. These could include shooting firearms, rock climbing, playing the piano, speaking a foreign language, ice skating, or skiing.
4. If you are aiming for roles in film or television, having experience in theatre productions, whether school, community, or professional theatre, is advantageous. Experience as an extra or background actor in films, comercials, or television can also be beneficial.
5. Starting with a resume, regardless of its length, is a positive step. Begin by listing any productions you've participated in and categorize them into sections like film, television, theatre, commercials, etc., based on your experience. Don't forget to include any experience from school or community theatre or any other productions you've been a part of. You can find the appropriate format for an Actor's resume online.
6. Always include a *Special Skills* section in your resume. You might possess a unique skill that could be sought after for specific projects.
7. Having a headshot, a professional photograph of your face, can be beneficial for Agents to visualize you. Initially, you could use a high-quality photo taken by someone you know. The agency will likely request more professional photos later, but at least they can get an idea of how you appear in photographs. If you already have a headshot, bring it to your interview.

8. Be ready to read sides (selected lines and paragraphs from a full script) during your interview. Agents often hold open calls where all interested parties must wait their turn to be called. They may ask you to read (perform the lines) or recite a memorized monologue.
9. A monologue, as defined by Merriam Webster, *is a dramatic sketch performed by a single actor*. You can find various monologues online for use.
10. A DVD of any films or projects you've participated in can be beneficial. This is professionally referred to as a reel, which is a compilation of your film/television work. Currently, Actors are using clips categorized by genre, such as drama, comedy, horror, etc., more than reels. As a beginner, you may not have this, which is why the initial items on this list are crucial.
11. If you're just starting out, it's best to find an agency open to working with beginners. Don't expect to sign with a top agency right away as they have high expectations and require professional reels/clips. Start small and gradually work your way up!
12. Seek advice from people already in the industry for agency recommendations. Be cautious as there are many scams in this business. You can research agencies online to determine their credibility. If they demand a fee to represent you, steer clear. All Agents do take an agency fee of 10 to 20% of the work you do, but they only get paid when you do. Typically, a 10% fee applies if you're union and 20% if you're nonunion. As a beginner, you won't be union.
13. Some agencies may try to charge you a significant amount for classes. If they make this a condition for signing you, avoid them. Evaluate this carefully. Some Agents offer reasonably priced classes on a voluntary basis. Seek your own training from theatre groups or community theatre that offers affordable classes. Casting Directors and some professional Actors also offer classes. You'll need to do your research and ask other Actors for recommendations.

With Burt Reynolds on set of Elbow Grease now titled An Innocent Kiss.

With Danny Sewell at the Cool Carolina Nights Red Carpet Gala.

Hair and Make-up on the set of Junebug.

With McLaurin Hull on the set of Junebug.

With Keith Harris and Owen Daly on the set of Fever Dreams: It's My House.

With Owen Daly on the set of Fever Dreams: It's My House.

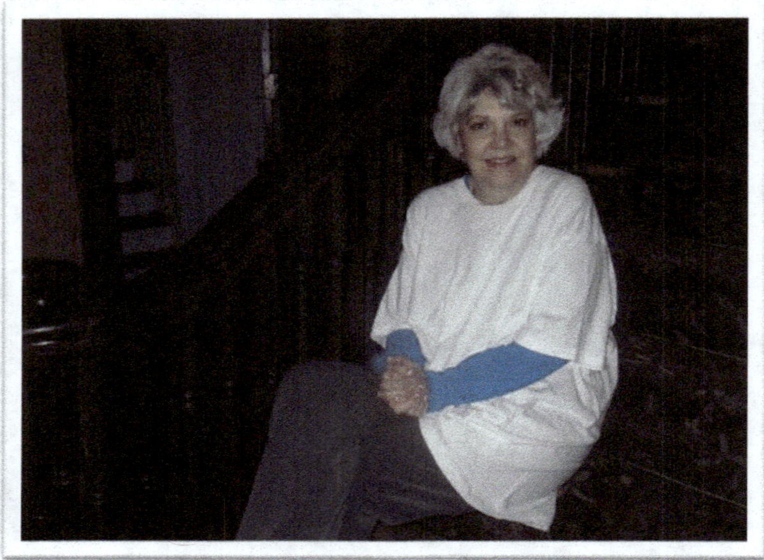

Catherine on the set of Main Street in Durham, NC

Catherine and Jason Damico walking the red carpet at the Peak City Film Festival in Apex, NC. (2nd quote)

JUNEBUG

"The beautifully acted film distills antagonistic red-state, blue-state attitudes... Ms. Adams's portrayal of an effusive girl-child is especially outstanding, and the camera's leisurely exploration of the family house conveys a rich, indelible sense of place."

"It is only a matter of time before Phil Morrison achieves the status of Jim Jarmusch, Gus Van Sant and Woody Allen."

"Amy Adams is a revelation!"

DIRECTED BY PHIL MORRISON

SONY PICTURES CLASSICS

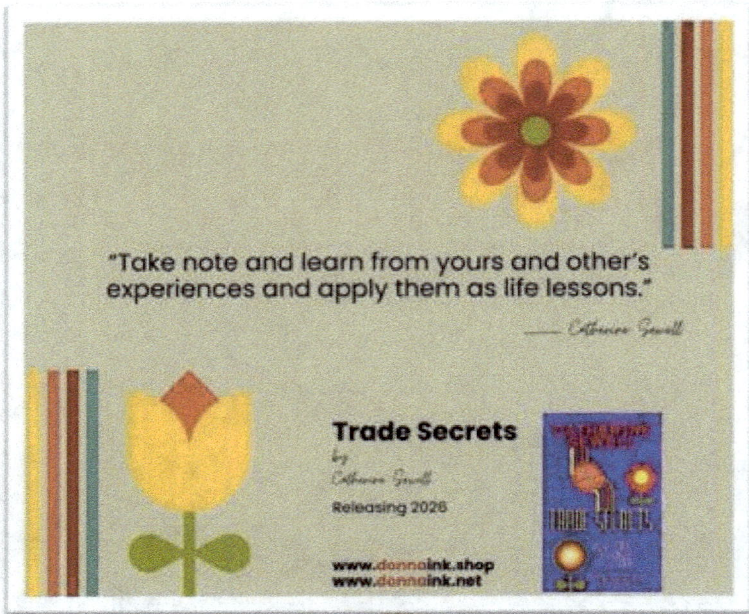
"Take note and learn from yours and other's experiences and apply them as life lessons."
— Catherine Sewell
Trade Secrets
by
Catherine Sewell
Releasing 2026
www.donnaink.shop
www.donnaink.net

"Imagination is everything.
It is the preview of life's coming attractions."
— Albert Einstein
Trade Secrets
by
Catherine Sewell
Releasing 2026
www.donnaink.shop
www.donnaink.net

CHAPTER EIGHTEEN

IT'S FINALLY HAPPENING (2017)

The year kicked off in a familiar fashion, with me doing background work on a commercial and continuing my role in an independent film project titled *Losing My Soul.* The filming took place in Wilmington, which was conveniently close for me.

I appeared in approximately thirteen episodes, and the Director expressed that my character was one of the favorites. This feedback was a boost to my confidence in my acting abilities. Every project, regardless of its size, contributes to your growth as an actor. Often, on-set training is more cost-effective than enrolling in expensive classes. Occasionally, you can use footage for a reel or clips showcasing your work.

Spring ushered in a unique and thrilling opportunity. A friend from Louisiana informed me about a play written by her friend, seeking Actors for a stage performance in New Or-leans. This was an attractive prospect as I was looking to gain more contemporary on-stage experience, given that most of my background was in film and television. I recorded a video audition for the Writer/Director, Mary Ann Sadler, and was thrilled when she cast me. The next task was to memorize my lengthy monologue.

The subsequent challenge was figuring out my travel arrangements. The idea of driving thirteen to fourteen hours to Louisiana alone was daunting, especially since my husband couldn't accompany me this time. I have a fear of flying, which hasn't been addressed since our flight to Colorado Springs during 9-11, when we were stranded for a day or so. We had to rent a car to return to North Carolina, and we were fortunate to do so. With no flights departing and my reluctance to board another plane, flying to Louisiana was ruled out. I explored the option of traveling via Amtrak. The coach fare was reasonable, so I decided to proceed with this option.

My desire to participate in this production was strong, especially considering I had never traveled on Amtrak before and would be doing so alone. But it was spring, a beautiful time of the year, so I was optimistic. The journey there was pleasant, with me enjoying solitude for most of the trip. However, sleeping at night proved challenging. We finally arrived at the *New Orleans Union Terminal* the following afternoon, having departed from Greensboro the previous evening. My friend, Susie Labry, was there to pick me up, a sight for sore eyes. The trip was enjoyable, filled with rehearsals every day and new friendships formed from the play. I didn't get much time for sightseeing, but the play went well, and I was pleased with my performance. MaryAnn recorded the performance, *His Wonderful Presence Then and Now,* which I revisited later.

When it was time to leave, Susie drove me back to New Orleans to catch the train. We arrived a bit late, and the queue was so long that I couldn't get processed in time. A kind individual at the station suggested another town where the train stops, so we hurriedly drove there. We had to wait for a while before the train arrived, which was nerve-wracking. The train was crowded, but I initially sat next to a pleasant man. Our conversation took a dark turn when he shared a tragic story about his son, after which he switched trains.

I was then joined by a man who reeked of alcohol and body odor and wouldn't stop talking. I took a break to dine in the dining car, providing temporary relief from the smell. Upon returning, I noticed a friendly-looking woman sitting alone. I decided to switch seats, even if it wasn't allowed. She agreed, much to my relief. However, I soon realized I had traded one unpleasant smell for another. The woman was nice, and our conversation was enjoyable, but she had been traveling on the train for over three days from California, which explained a lot. I figured out that she must be wearing an adult diaper, or she had an accident, because the odor was almost unbearable. I almost got sick on my stomach! Well, then I was stuck for a long time until she changed trains. I finally arrived in Greensboro around 1:00 or 2:00 the next morning. I learned from this trip if I ever go by Amtrak again, it won't be at a coach fare. You get what you pay for sooner or later!!! *See, I told you that every event or production is a learning experience!*

What an eventful spring and summer it was! In May, I secured a role in *Homicide Hunter*, which is broadcasted on the Investigation *Discovery Channel* (ID). I've mentioned this in the docudramas chapter earlier.

The filming took place in Knoxville, Tennessee. So, just a month after my challenging train journey back from Louisiana, I found myself on the road again. Interestingly, I had to travel to yet another state about two months later for a project named, *Boosterthon 2017 – Teacher Meeting*. This was a pep rally-style fundraising program used in schools. I portrayed a humorous character, *Teacher / Mrs. Clark*. The amusing aspect of this video was that the teachers behaved like students. The filming occurred in Roswell, Georgia, an area of Atlanta that I enjoyed exploring. While it was exciting, it was also amusing how things seemed to happen simultaneously or close together. I relished this project as it allowed me to showcase my comedic skills. Even the crew found my performance amusing. Just a few days after returning home, I received a callback for an audition I had done earlier. Guess where it was? Back to Georgia again! Such is the life of an actor.

As August rolled in, I wrapped up the film project, "Losing My Soul" I was working on in the Wilmington area. Thankfully, this project was in the same state I reside in.

My next transformative experience began on August 22, 2017, with the rehearsal of *Footloose* for the *Temple Theatre* in Sanford, North Carolina. My NC talent Agent believed it would be beneficial for me to gain more theatre experience, which was one reason I participated in the play in Louisiana. Before the Louisiana play, I had only done one other play, a staged reading called *Bark*, written by Grace Ellis and directed by Vicki King. This staged play was performed in the middle of an apple orchard on an outdoor stage in the picturesque mountain area of Cana, Virginia.

So, *Footloose* was my third venture into theater. My third foray into theatre was unlike my previous two experiences. I auditioned earlier in the summer and was granted a spot in the ensemble of *Footloose*. I thought it would just involve singing, which I love. However, as a theatre novice, I soon discovered it involved more than just singing. I had to dance and remember the sequence of dance steps. It wasn't long before I questioned my decision to "experience theatre" as a change from film.

I must express my deep respect for theatre Actors. I don't think I've ever worked and moved as much in my entire life. The rehearsals were long, lasting hours, days, and weeks! But by the time we performed the play, I knew what to sing, when to sing, where to dance, and when to dance. I even found my-self dancing on the platform, despite my age! Everything went well, and I managed not to trip. As it turned out, I chose to participate in the play that became the theatre's biggest box office hit over the years. This made me proud! Our Director, Peggy Taphorn, is wonderful. She gave me a chance despite my limited experience. *Will I try another large production like this one again?* Only time will tell.

The fall of 2017 continued with other projects like commercials and a small independent film. The local film, *Copper Sky*, was a cowboy movie written and directed by Ron Koontz and filmed in Sanford, NC, in a cowboy town built by Tim Marsh. This was also where I filmed a movie Tim wrote and directed, which I mentioned in an earlier chapter. I had a lead role in this one and gained more experience by having to learn a lot of script. My husband and grandson were given small parts. This was our grandson's first introduction to film. He loved it and wanted to continue. I share the sentiment of some other Actors who say, *If you can choose any other profession than acting, then do it.* That logic didn't work very well for me though! I suppose if acting is the only career you want, and you are determined and have a thick skin; don't mind hearing "no" many, many times, then go for it.

In November, I received news from Mary Ann Sadler, the Writer and Director of the *play His Wonderful Presence Then and Now,* which I had performed back in April. She informed all of us involved in the production the video of the play was ready for viewing, scheduled for December 10, 2017. I was thrilled it was completed and looked forward to traveling to New Orleans to watch it.

Shortly after hearing about the screening, I received some fantastic news from my Louisiana Agents, the Landrums. I had secured a role in a union feature horror film called *Darlin'*, set to be filmed in the Baton Rouge area. I was ecstatic about being cast in this film, which fortuitously was filming in December. This allowed me to attend the video screening of the play and participate in the film within a two-week timeframe.

My friend, Susie Labry, generously offered her home for me to stay during this period. Susie, also in the business, made it special to share these experiences together. While I had a place to stay upon arrival, the question remained: *How was I going to get there?* I was apprehensive about flying, the drive was too long to undertake alone, and the train held unpleasant memories. I preferred to drive but didn't want to make such a long journey by myself. My husband couldn't accompany me, and my cousin by marriage, Mary Ayers, who often travels with me, didn't want to travel that far either.

So, what was my next move? I decided to check flight rates and found a reasonably priced flight that required only one plane change. It was even less expensive than the train if I opted for business class or a cabin. I decided to face my fears and seize both great opportunities. In this business, you must grab opportunities when they present themselves. Years ago, one of my acting instructors told us that we could find work if we were willing to leave our comfort zones. He was right. Most of my significant roles have been in states other than my own.

The flights to and from were both smooth with no turbulence. Susie greeted me at the airport, and to our surprise, it snowed heavily on our way to her house. It was almost like a blizzard. Susie was thrilled, as they rarely see such heavy snowfall in Louisiana. I wasn't as enthusiastic, given we had to endure the snow for about a week. We're more accustomed to snow in North Carolina.

I had an entire week to explore, attend Christmas parties like the *Louisiana Film Industry Party*, listen to Susie and other church members perform *Handel's Messiah*, participate in other Christmas events, and attend a film screening, among other things. One of the highlights was attending the *Legislative*

Christmas Party at the state capital in Baton Rouge. Susie had an invitation and was able to bring me along. I enjoyed dressing up and mingling with the political elites! I even had the opportunity to meet Governor Jon Bel Edwards, something I haven't even done in North Carolina.

This trip was a unique opportunity for me to enjoy myself beyond just traveling to my work location and returning home. I also managed to work on two additional film projects while waiting to work on *Darlin'* on December 20. The pro-projects, *Green Book* and *The Devils Hitching Post*, provided exciting experiences. On the day we worked on *Green Book*, we shared a restaurant scene with renowned Actors Maher-shala Ali and Viggo Mortensen.

The second film was shot in a western town in the Baton Rouge area, the same location where *The Magnificent Seven* (2016) with Denzel Washington was filmed. In the film, Susie and I played churchgoers, thoroughly enjoying ourselves dressing in period wardrobe and participating in a singing scene. Jonah Monet directed the film, with Jency Griffin Hogan as the Co-Director. Both also had roles in the film.

AUTHOR ANNOTATIONS & GOOD TO KNOWS

This chapter certainly told of some of my most challenging experiences in trying to reach my goals and dreams. I certainly had to face my fears of flying or miss the opportunity. It was just that simple. Also, I had to learn by stark experience that others don't always have the same lifestyles or values I have. There again, all of this was a learning experience and opportunity to learn from the sometimes cruel or uncomfortable situations in life.

On my Louisiana trip, I was able to experience two different lifestyles. I had the opportunity to experience the extravagance of the elite or let's say the economically enriched lifestyles of the politically advantaged. I admit it was exciting to have this opportunity. My goal is to try to adapt as a chameleon to whatever environment I encounter, as long as it aligns with my values.

ACTOR TRAINING INSIGHTS & TIDBITS

Key Points To Consider

1. Plan for the unexpected where possible! Try to envision what could go wrong and what you could do in that situation. Opportunities develop quickly and you need to be prepared. Example: Acquiring a Passport.
2. Be prepared to travel if you want to take advantage of more opportunities. Transportation is an important aspect of the business. Hope you are comfortable with air flight. The majority of the times you will probably be able to just drive. So, practical preparation is to have dependable transportation.

One of the biggest warnings I gave in an earlier chapter is getting scammed by people claiming to be able to cast you in a film. The first thing they do is to ask for money! Always research out any talent agency, acting school etc. first to be sure they are legit. No legit talent agency or casting agency will charge you. Training in most cases, whether a school or individual will charge. However, still research their qualifications before considering them.

With Danny Sewell (my husband) and Gavan Dowdy (my grandson) on the set of Copper Sky.

One of the many "Sold Out" performances of Footloose.

"It's a wrap" on Footloose.

With Susie Labry at the Louisiana Film Industry Christmas Party.

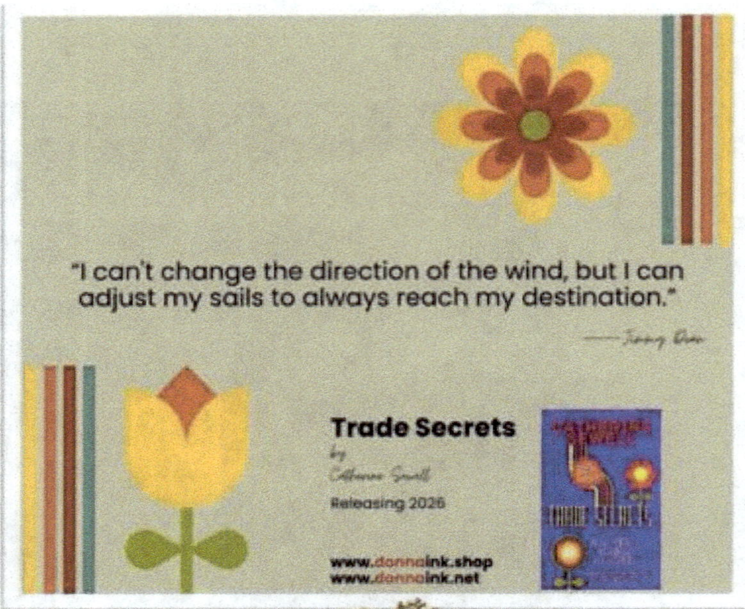
"I can't change the direction of the wind, but I can adjust my sails to always reach my destination."
Trade Secrets
Releasing 2026
www.donnaink.shop
www.donnaink.net

"You miss 100% of the shots you don't take."
Trade Secrets
Releasing 2026
www.donnaink.shop
www.donnaink.net

CHAPTER NINETEEN

BRING THOSE AUDITIONS ON! (2018-2019)

The year 2018 began as an avalanche of auditions. I thought from the way the year started out I was going to really nab a great project. Many Actors just hope and pray for the auditions to come. That is the first necessary step in the process to book the gig. I have certainly been fortunate and blessed with a wide variety of impressive television, film and commercial auditions. These popular projects seemed to be even more impressive and forthcoming this year. The downside to this is; the more impressive and popular the project is, the more competitive the competition is. On some of the auditions, I had the privilege of getting a callback. A callback is when you are among a select few that are strongly considered for the role. In other words, any of the candidates would be able to handle the role. This is when they start having to 'weed out' the Actors by some preference and there will be negotiating going on for each person's choice. Even though I didn't book some of these biggest projects this year, I felt I must be becoming a more competitive candidate since I am being asked to audition. In other words, someone in that negotiating room liked me and spoke positively of my work.

In a business that can be very frustrating and disappointing, you are better off looking at the subtleties that indicate progress and accomplishment. Several of the remote auditions I did and felt so good about, I didn't even hear from them for a callback. Sometimes it is really hard to figure out. This goes to show you how good the competition is. However, there are many factors that enter into an actor being booked or not. Oftentimes, whether you are hired or not may have little to do with whether you are the most talented or not. Your age range, weight, height, hair, personality, and location, plus many more reasons, could be why an actor doesn't book.

You just try to learn from the experience and say "next." It is often helpful to watch the television show or film you auditioned for and see who was cast. That can give you a clue as to what they had in mind for the role. Chances are you see why they were selected.

For each role in a project, there is a breakdown of the character. This breakdown gives a simple description of what they want the character to look like and their personality. An example may be that the Casting Director is looking for a tall, skinny Caucasian female with a British accent and a bubbly personality. If you watch the show and see the actor they chose had a more natural British accent, then you may be able to figure out why you weren't cast. Sometimes it isn't easy.

It is crazy but sometimes you may not get the role because you looked like the Director's mother-in-law, which he/she doesn't like or you reminded the Director/Producer of his ex-spouse. There are many reasons. as I mentioned earlier, why you may not get cast. All you can do is to prepare for the audition and call back and be the best you can be. Then move on to the next opportunity and don't look back!

The year began with work on a *Nascar Commercial* in Mooresville, NC. My role was as a receptionist sitting behind a large counter desk in the office building room. The exciting part is, I had the opportunity to interact with Bubba Wallace in the scene plus being in the room with numerous Nascar drivers. When the commercial came out, I was just a blur sitting behind the counter desk. Nevertheless, I had fun that day, especially being around all those handsome famous men, and got paid too! In early 2019, I was in a *Nascar Hall of Fame* project as a Grandma in an extra role.

This year I worked on two *Bojangle Commercials* as an extra. One was in the winter, and the other, in the springtime. Both commercials were in Charlotte, NC where the *Bojangle*

Restaurants Chain originated. There was a quick view of me on both of them. In the summer of 2019, I worked in Hunters-ville, NC in a *Food Lion Commercial* as a featured customer.

Following the above commercials, came the *Cone Health Medical Hospital Commercial* in the fall. This was filmed in Charlotte, and I was a birthday party attendee. I had the added fun benefit of my husband Danny working on this one with me. For someone not too interested in working in the industry, Danny surely is advancing along and learning how the business works. Doing background/extra work is a great opportunity to see firsthand how the industry works.

Yet another *Food Lion Commercial* opportunity was for a Food Lion in Huntersville, NC. I was a featured extra customer. I just love the chance to travel to different cities in NC working on commercials, as otherwise; I may not ordinarily travel to. I occasionally work out of state on commercials but mostly am employed to work right here in NC.

Some North Carolina films were produced right in my neck of the woods. The first of these was *Copper Sky,* a Ron Koontz's film. I played the lead role of Norror and worked in various crew roles in this Western. My husband, Danny, had a lead role, and worked on the crew, also.

Another film I had a role in was *Jailhouse Wedding,* writ-ten and produced by Perry Ball. It was filmed in Raleigh, NC. In September of 2019, I played the role of Deputy Laura King in a scene with the lead Robert Goodwin. I enjoyed playing a deputy, as I've never had a role like this one before.

Yet another film project in 2019 was called *The Coward.* It was written by Dean Pyles. I played the role of a Granny and Danny got to be an extra. The exciting part of this film was we traveled to Alexander City, Alabama to film. Neither Danny nor I had ever been there before. We stayed in a beautiful B&B home which we both enjoyed. This was the second time during my career I had the fun opportunity to stay in a B&B home. I love old homes so both were special.

My husband, Danny, and I had another fun opportunity to work together. The location was the beautiful Lake Lure in North Carolina. This project was for tourism in Rutherford County, NC. In one of the shots, we sat on the deck of the *Lake Lure Club House* overlooking the lake. Other shots were in one of the rental houses on site. How enjoyable and got paid for it 'to boot'.

Every once in a while, an unusual, or out of the ordinary job opportunity comes along. Danny and I were cast to work on a project called *Above and Beyond* for the *Passion City Church* in Atlanta, Georgia. Danny and I went all the way to Atlanta to slow dance together overlooking a section of the city. Once again, more fun working an easy job in an interesting city. How much I have enjoyed being able to work with my husband on many projects. In addition to our being together, another good side-line of our working together is, we get double pay!

Another title of this chapter could have been an avalanche of re-enactments/docudramas. A goodly number of opportunities surfaced for these shows during this 2018-2019 time period. Four out of a total of five were crime shows, which were filmed in Knoxville, Tennessee. Three of the shows were filmed in 2019, so I kept the road hot to Knoxville. The crime show *Homicide for the Holidays* brought me to the end of the year of work for 2019. These specific TV crime series are referenced in *Chapter 14* on *Documentary, Reenactments / Docudramas.*

AUTHOR ANNOTATIONS & GOOD TO KNOWS

This two-year period was exciting and eventful. I was invited to audition for some high budget *SAG-AFTRA* movie projects. The audition opportunities gave me some validation of my acting skills and encouragement for the future. In this business, auditioning is certainly seen as work. If you don't do the work and give it your best, then don't expect to receive invites to auditions. Technology knowledge for self-taping is an important component of the selection process. If they can't see you well or hear you, then they will just delete the audition.

The longer you persist in this industry; you may have some totally different chances to work on some 'out of the ordinary' projects. This is like spicing up your food; it keeps the work exciting and fun.

Actor Training Insights & Tidbits

Key Points To Consider

In most cases you will need an Agent in order to audition for film, commercials, industrial/training films and some other type projects. For small independent films you may be able to audition without an Agent by submitting yourself for the project. You still need to fit the breakdown description of the role.

1. ***What is a breakdown description of roles?***

   A breakdown description is a document that describes the characters, roles, and requirements for production. It is used to communicate with Actors, their Agents, and Managers what is needed during the casting process. It provides important information for Agents / Managers to know which Actors to submit and also lets the Actors evaluate whether they are suitable for a particular role. It is a standardized format for Agent or Manager submissions.

2. ***Some key components of the breakdown include the following***: a summary of the project, character descriptions like gender, ethnicity, age range, physical specifics like height, hair color, and a description of the character's personality.

   Other components include instructions on how to submit, the location of filming, whether travel or accommodations are provided, and whether cast, pay information, and any other additional information required for the role.

   Examples of this may be dialects, fluency in a language, and a specific sport skill like soccer.

3. ***What are sides?***

   Sides are an excerpt taken from a script. It could be a few lines, one or more pages, or a whole scene. The actor is expected to perform these sides at a live audition or when self-taping. Usually, the sides are provided to you by your Agent or Manager. Oftentimes, the sides are posted on *Sides Express*, which is a division of *Breakdown Services*.

Basic Auditioning Tips

1. Use eye contact with the person you are communicating with.
2. Learn to really hear what the other actor is saying to you. This is needed to appear realistic.
3. Read your sides thoroughly and fully comprehend what is being said.
4. When speaking, what you do with the words and phrases in the text are an important acting skill. Our language is an important tool, so learn to understand the meaning-the obvious and the more abstruse. Learn to use variety in your voice so it doesn't come across as flat; but sounds real when you deliver a line.
5. Establish and develop a strong character and learn what the transformations or changes your character should make in the scene. Read and study about techniques and ways to do this.
6. It is important to 'take a moment before', so to speak, before beginning your first line. There is always some action that precedes your first line (e.g.: You may be eating or reading the newspaper or just thinking).
7. The structure of the story/performance you are relaying has a beginning, middle and end.
8. It is important to learn more than one way to perform a scene. Casting may request that you perform a scene two different ways for the audition.
9. Have fun with your read (audition) and relax! Pretend you are talking with your best friend.

Catherine Sewell as a Granny and Danny Sewell as an extra.

"Change is inevitable. Growth is optional."
—John Maxwell
Trade Secrets
Releasing 2026
www.donnaink.shop
www.donnaink.net

"By failing to prepare, you are preparing to fail."
Trade Secrets
Releasing 2026
www.donnaink.shop
www.donnaink.net

CHAPTER TWENTY

THE COVID YEARS (2020-2023)

On March 11, 2020, COVID-19 was declared by the *World Health Organization* (WHO) as a global pandemic. The *Centers for Disease Control* (CDC) stated, "COVID-19 (coronavirus disease 2019) is a disease caused by the SARS-CoV-2 virus and most often causes respiratory symptoms that can feel much like a cold, the flu, or pneumonia. COVID-19 may attack more than your lungs and respiratory system." (CDC website, 6-13-2020).

In an *ABC News* article, written by Mary Kekatos, COVID-19 Timeline: *How The Deadly Virus And The World's Response Have Evolved Over 4 Years*, an *ABC News COVID-19 Pandemic Timeline* was presented. The timeline of March 11, 2020, was given as the beginning date of the pandemic. "The WHO classifies Covid 19 as a pandemic." The ending timeline for Covid-19 was charted as May 11, 2023. The actual statement on the chart was, *The Public Health Emergency For COVID-19 Expires In The U.S.*, (Kekatos, Mary, ABC News, March 11, 2024)

The COVID-19 years had a devastating effect on my career, and I am sure it did for many other Actors also. It was essentially like my career was put on pause for almost 3-years. As I mentioned in an earlier chapter, I was receiving some real name film projects to audition for and was feeling optimistic about my future. COVID-19 came and knocked the wind out of my sails! Now it is taking me time to reestablish my reputation, skills and work ethic in the business. Just in the past two years, I have begun moving forward with a multitude of auditions. Some of the productions I worked for in the past and haven't reestablished a relationship with them yet. I am aware it will take more time to return to my previous status, if that is possible at this point. Oh my! I am three years older too. However, I am pleased it does appear that things are heading in a positive direction. I still have my great Agents.

It was a good thing I was able to work on two projects before COVID-19 was declared a global pandemic in March of 2020 as after that date things began to really crank up with restrictions, isolation and other mandates. Actors were just a small part of the population experiencing a loss of jobs and businesses. We were certainly "all in this together," but not from a positive standpoint.

The first project I worked on in 2020 was *It's Supernatural* with Sid Roth. This was the episode of Ryan Johnson in which I played the mother of Ryan Johnson who had cancer. This episode was mentioned in Chapter 14 on re-enactments. The other project was completed the day before March 11, 2020, global pandemic was declared. It was a project called *GA Power Heroes for Georgia Power*. My husband had a lead role as a granddad. I played his wife in the shot. How funny, I play-ed his wife! We enjoyed working on this together and having the chance to travel to Woodstock, Georgia.

In the summer months of July and August, I worked on two more commercials. One was for an *Auto Zone Commercial* as a customer and *Founders Federal Credit Union Commercial* as a patron. We filmed *Auto Zone* in Charlotte and *Founders Federal Credit Union* in Rock Hill, South Carolina. I always like to go to Rock Hill since it is in South Carolina, my home state, and especially to ride by and see *Winthrop University* where my Mother went to college. The name changed from *Winthrop College* to *Winthrop University* in 2001.

COVID-19 mandates such as masks, lockdowns, the COV-ID-19 vaccine and PCR testing were in full swing during the 2021–2022-time frame. *SAG-AFTRA* and the production companies were requiring the above in order for Actors to work. If you were cast in union and possibly some nonunion, you may have been required to be Polymerase Chain Reaction (PCR) tested two to three times each week you worked. The union projects would test you on site. Masks and the vax were also required for employment. My husband and I did have some auditions early on in 2021 but as the year progressed we declined to audition or work when the mandates became heavily enforced. We were both selected to have principal roles on a project for a *Health Care Commercial* but declined the opportunity. Both the years 2021, through most of 2022, were almost void of work until the end months of the year. Danny and I were both hired as a couple to work on an industrial/training video for *Aspen Dental* in Jacksonville, NC during the month of September. By then strict mandates were lifted and we completed this project and another one in the month of November for *The Legacy at North Augusta-A National Lutheran Community TV Commercial* recording. This commercial was filmed in Staunton, Virginia. We were happy to finally work again after almost two years. Both were interesting and different projects. Never had we done anything close to a dental clinic training video where my whole mouth was actually imaged in order to demonstrate use of the equip-ment.

Some reports indicated COVID-19's ending timeline was in May of 2023. However, the year started out with 2 auditions in January. Both of these were union film auditions for which there is significant competition from around the country. On neither invitation to audition was listed any COVID-19 mandates if cast for the roles. This may or may not mean if cast, they would be required at the time of filming. I did not book either one so I do not know what that status was. However, it seemed from these early months, some of the mandates such as masks and mandated vaccinations were less strict or laxed. More auditions didn't occur until spring with the majority of them coming in the summer months, mainly August. By this time frame, the mandates were no longer required by the unions or the production companies.

AUDITION & BOOKING REFLECTIONS: 2023–2025

The fall and winter audition season of 2023, spanning September through December, averaged about one audition per month. In truth, when I look at the entire year, the pattern was the same: roughly one audition per month. It was a hard year for landing gigs, and many Actors experienced similar challenges as the industry continued its slow recovery.

Bookings in 2024 were also uneventful. I'm still examining the reasons behind that lull, and I encourage every actor to do the same when their momentum shifts. The post-pandemic years (2024 and 2025) were transitional for many of us, and while 2024 was quiet, things began picking up again in 2025. I'll be sharing more about that renewed activity in a future edition.

When bookings slow down, it's important to pause and take an honest, compassionate look at what might be contributing to the change. I began by asking myself a series of questions and then sought input from my Agents and other trusted professsionals. Some Agents are more hands-on than others, and many stay so busy the responsibility often falls on the Actor to initiate the conversation. Still, reaching out for pro-fessional eyes on your auditions, taping setup, and overall presentation can be invaluable. Here are some of the questions I asked myself:

1. How much did my frustration or emotional fatigue from the pandemic years affect my performance, energy, or temperament in auditions?
2. Was my appearance — hairstyle, wardrobe choices, or overall presentation — aligned with the roles I was submitting for? Did my audition skills need refreshing?
3. Had production companies shifted their expectations or casting preferences compared to pre-pandemic norms?
4. Were my filming and self-taping skills up to current industry standards?
5. Was it time to update my camera, lighting, or other taping equipment?

These questions led to even more reflection, and the process itself became a form of professional reset. Here's to a stronger, more aligned, and more productive 2025 — and beyond.

Author Annotations And Good-To-Knows

Life has a way of throwing unexpected curves that can shift our direction or challenge our confidence. What matters most is staying grounded in your beliefs and not allowing public pressure or outside noise to dictate your path. Seek truth in every situation. Don't accept everything you hear or read as fact. *Think it through. Question it. Explore it.*

The Socratic Method — a dialogue built on thoughtful questioning — can be a powerful tool for Actors and for life. There are many helpful videos online that break down how his approach works and how we can apply it to our own decision-making and self-reflection.

Actor Training Insights And Tidbits

Key Points to Consider

1. Commercial auditioning requires a distinct skill set. Understanding the unique delivery style and expectations of commercial work is essential for consistent bookings.
2. Mark Brandon, in *Winning Auditions: 101 Strategies for Actors* (2005), identifies three primary types of commercials: (For deeper insight, refer to his book.)
   a) **Product-Spokesperson Commercial** - You and the product are the focus. Your job is to sell with authority, determination , and warmth. Some spots require more warmth than others. Dress in a way that supports the tone of the commercial.

   b) **Slice-of-Life Commercial** - These portray everyday activities — shopping, cooking, dining out, playing with children or grandchildren. Dialogue may be minimal or nonexistent. What matters is natural behavior, ease, and a pleasant, relatable presence.

   c) **Classic Spot** - This longstanding format presents a problem and positions the product as the solution. For example, face cream reduces wrinkles or acne. These spots require emotional progression: frustration or dissatisfaction at the start, followed by relief and satisfaction once the product is introduced.

- **Study the storyboard carefully** if one is provided. Analyze the sides using the techniques above.
- **Dress appropriately for the audition type.** For example, you wouldn't wear a business suit for a kitchen-cooking scenario.

SID ROTH
IT'S SUPERNATURAL!
WELCOME TO MY WORLD, WHERE IT'S
NATURALLY SUPERNATURAL

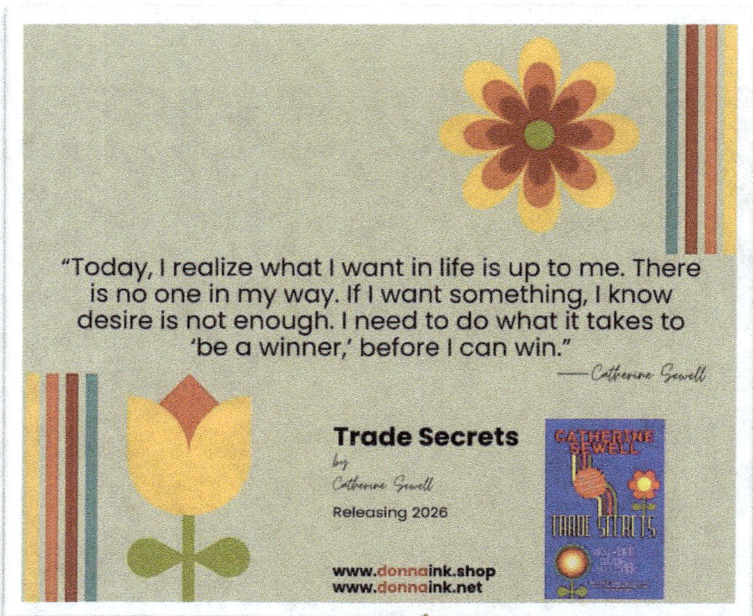
"Today, I realize what I want in life is up to me. There is no one in my way. If I want something, I know desire is not enough. I need to do what it takes to 'be a winner,' before I can win."
—Catherine Sewell
Trade Secrets
by
Catherine Sewell
Releasing 2026
www.donnaink.shop
www.donnaink.net
CATHERINE SEWELL
TRADE SECRETS

"Building a habit of acknowledgment — through notes, referrals, or public mentions — strengthens your relationships and reinforces the collaborative spirit of the craft."
—Catherine Sewell
Trade Secrets
by
Catherine Sewell
Releasing 2026
www.donnaink.shop
www.donnaink.net
CATHERINE SEWELL
TRADE SECRETS

CHAPTER TWENTY-ONE

CONCLUSION

My career in the entertainment industry has spanned more than two decades, and I hope you've found this journey as enjoyable as I have. If you are contemplating or planning your own venture into this industry, I hope my experiences and business insights have been enlightening. As a trained teacher, I'm always eager to share knowledge that could potentially make your experiences smoother or more rewarding. After all, once a teacher, always a teacher!

It is astounding how many new skills I have had to acquire to broaden my opportunities. *It is all about confronting your fears, believing in yourself, and taking the plunge*.

The thought of performing in theatre and on stage was nerve-wracking for me, having spent so long in film and television. However, I pushed myself to try it, to boost my confidence and expand my skill set. Ralph Waldo Emerson put it best when he said, "He hasn't learned the lesson of life who does not every day surmount a fear." Surmount your fears!

While most people start with theatre, I chose a different path. Now, I have had a variety of experiences and can make more informed choices for the future. I believe most people tend to concentrate on certain aspects of business, and rightly so, as it is challenging to master everything. Your specific skills, interests, physical health, age, markets, and location all influence what you choose to focus on. There are some roles you

simply cannot play or play well, and Casting Directors will help determine that by not selecting you for an audition.

Some of the highlights of my experiences were not necessarily speaking roles or high-paying jobs. I particularly enjoyed my stand-in work as it allowed me to interact closely with some major stars.

Having the opportunity to observe how they work was insightful. *Divine Secrets of the Ya-Ya Sisterhood* and *Main Street* were my favorite stand-in jobs. I have enjoyed doing extra work for similar reasons, though not to the same extent as stand-in work. One perk of extra / background work is you sometimes get seen. For instance, I recently appeared briefly in two *Bojangles' TV Commercials*. As I mentioned earlier, commercials tend to pay better than film work for background roles.

However, the pay was not the reason, I wanted to be an extra at the start of my career. If you enjoy the business as I do, then most work can be enjoyable. A noteworthy point about extra/background work is you do not need an Agent to get work. There are several websites on the Internet where you can become a member for free, and some require membership to submit yourself for work. Some of these sites also allow you to submit for an audition for principal speaking roles. However, your chances of getting those are better if an Agent submits you for the audition.

Warnings are a crucial part of this business due to the prevalence of scams. Before signing with an agency, do an Internet search to check their reputation and/or ask other Actors. There are also websites where Actors report scams. If they ask you for money to sign you, then steer clear. Also, be wary if they promise you work.

One of the biggest scams in my early years were Agents encouraging you to use a specific photographer who charged a high price. The Agent would naturally get substantial kickbacks from the photographer. It's less expensive to find and hire one yourself. Ask others in the business for recommendations. You can often see samples of photographers' works online. There are other types of scams out there, so just be careful. If it sounds too good to be true, then it probably is. This cliché is always a good one to keep in mind.

If your main goals to enter the entertainment business are fame and fortune, then don't even bother. Unless you are the child of a famous star, have contacts in high places, or just get lucky and hit a film that becomes a big hit - chances are slim you will achieve fame and fortune. Now, if you are interested in storytelling and having fun, then you should reach those goals. No one knows who will become a star, so there is no playbook or manual that can tell you how.

Even to be a working actor and enjoy some success, you really must put in the work. Training is important to success, just as it is for any vocation you choose. Remember, this is a business, and professionals expect you to be one. That takes training and practice. The more you train and take classes, the more you realize there is still so much to learn. Even seasoned Actors regularly train and attend classes. Acting might seem easy, and you might think it is all about delivering lines; but that's not the case. It's challenging to appear natural and present in the moment. Even one-liners can be tough to nail. In fact, I have even read about classes that train Actors for just 'one-liners.'

If Acting has always been your dream and passion, pursue it. Don't let concerns about your age, appearance, person-ality, contacts, or skills hold you back. Remember, success is subject-tive. It varies from person to person. Some might not consider themselves successful unless they achieve stardom. Others might feel successful if they land a role in a television show, film, or play. The definition of success is personal. Personally, I feel successful, even though I am not rich and famous. I enjoy storytelling and embracing new challenges. The more unconventional the role is, the more challenging and enjoyable it is for me. I still have goals I'd like to achieve even after twenty-plus years.

If there is one takeaway from this book for you, it is you should chase your dream regardless of your age or any self-imposed limitations. This applies to any career you aspire to. You can always start small and gradually dip your toes in the water. Everyone is here for a reason — to fulfill their destiny!

Whatever career you choose, make sure to enjoy the journey!

Happy trails until we meet again. May your journey be one of intent, purpose, enjoyment, and truth!

TOP THIRTEEN DOS FOR ENTERTAINMENT BUSINESS

1. Pursue your dreams.
2. Have faith in your abilities and maintain self-assurance.
3. Seek education in fields that interest you.
4. Build connections with others.
5. Show kindness and friendliness to everyone you encounter.
6. Maintain professionalism, as this *is a business environment.*
7. Learn to handle rejection gracefully.
8. Seek out opportunities on your own.
9. Starting with extra/background work is a good way to gain experience.
10. A professional headshot and resume are essential tools in this field.
11. Keep a positive attitude, as this can be a challenging industry.
12. Keep pushing forward, no matter what.
13. Persistence, tenacity, perseverance, and determination are keys to success.

TIPS ON FINDING WORK IN THE INDUSTRY

1. An Agent isn't always necessary for extra / background work. Some Agents may not handle film extra work, but might occasionally submit you for commercial extra work, which typically pays better than film.
2. Various acting/entertainment websites are a good source for finding extra work and some principal work. While some of these sites offer free memberships with limited services, others charge a fee for full access and premium services.

3. Facebook can be a valuable resource for job hunting. By connecting with Casting Directors and production companies, you can stay updated on their project needs.

4. *The Wilmywood Daily* on Facebook provides casting information and other useful acting resources for the Wilmington, NC, area.

5. Some websites may offer casting information, such as:

   a) Actors Access, Casting Networks, and

   b) 800 Casting

   They may also require membership fees or charge for credential submissions for audition consideration. Agents can submit on behalf of the Actors they represent at no cost on these websites. You can also self-submit.

6. Networking with other Actors, Casting Directors, and Entertainment Professionals is a great way to learn about potential job opportunities. I have been hired multiple times by friends and acquaintances in the business.

7. Attending film festivals, workshops, or conferences can provide opportunities to meet and network with others who are aware of upcoming projects.

8. Having a Talent Agent can significantly increase your audition and job opportunities. However, many Actors continue to seek auditions and work independently, even if they have an Agent. Most Agents appreciate seeing their Actors working and do not mind if Actors find some of their own work. The more work and experience you gain, the more marketable you become to your Agent. And when you acquire work yourself, let your Agent know.

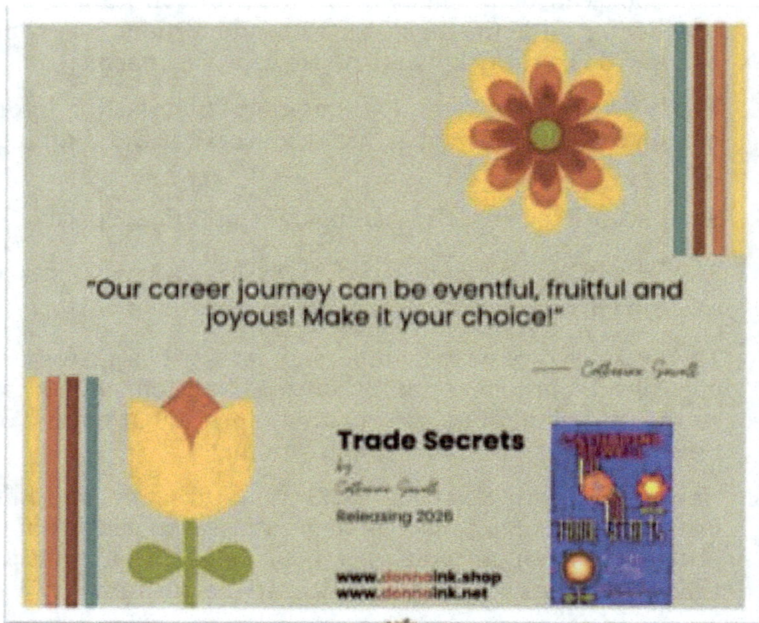
"Our career journey can be eventful, fruitful and joyous! Make it your choice!"
Trade Secrets
Releasing 2026
www.donnaink.shop
www.donnaink.net

"Every great dream begins with a dreamer. Always remember, you have within you the strength, the patience, and the passion to reach for the stars to change the world."
Trade Secrets
Releasing 2026
www.donnaink.shop
www.donnaink.net

THE INTEGRATION GUIDE

ACTOR DEVELOPMENT AND ASSESSMENT

INTEGRATION GUIDE OVERVIEW

Your journey as an actor is shaped by both your inner world and the practical steps you take to develop your craft. *The Integration Guide* is designed to help you bring those two dimensions together. Through reflection, self-assess-ment, and intentional action, you will begin to understand not only *where you are* in your artistic development, but also *where you are headed.*

This guidebook functions as a companion to your training. It offers space to explore your motivations, acknowledge the people who have influenced your path, and build the habits and systems that support long-term growth. Each section in-vites you to slow down, reflect deeply, and then move for-ward with clarity and purpose.

You will encounter prompts, checklists, and open-ended questions throughout these pages. They are not tests, nor are they meant to be rushed. Instead, they serve as touchpoints to pause, notice what is emerging, and document your evolving understanding of yourself as an artist.

As you progress, you will move from reflection into act-ion, from inner awareness into practical application. This structure mirrors the actor's process itself: grounding, discovery, and expression.

With that foundation in place, you are ready to begin.

PART I— Mentors and Guides

No actor gets where they are going alone. Behind every performance are mentors, teachers, and coaches who have poured time, energy, and belief into an actor's growth. Saying thank you is not just polite — it is a way of honoring those relationships and keeping them alive.

As you begin this journey as a student of the arts, you are invited to move from reflection into practical action. Identifying the mentors and motivators who have shaped you helps create a foundation where personal growth and real-world experience meet—and, over time, evolve into genuine expertise. Honoring this transition through both reflection and action strengthens your skills and builds essential resilience.

The Integration Guide is designed to function as your workbook. Each question in this section is followed by either three blank lines or check boxes. The lines offer space for your written responses; the boxes allow you to quickly mark what applies. Take your time with each prompt. With honesty and integrity, name both industry and non-industry individuals who have helped or influenced you. Capture insights as they surface. This is your personal record and a meaningful first step in integrating your artistic development with your lived experience.

So, take a breath, gather your thoughts, and move into the questions ahead. Use your emerging insights to begin defining—and expand your artistic voyage here.

Identify Your Mentors and Motivators

Every artist is shaped by the people who walk beside them. Some offer guidance, some offer challenge, and some offer a single moment of encouragement that changes everything. Identifying your mentors and motivators helps you understand the influences that have shaped your artistic voice and the support systems that continue to sustain your growth.

This section invites you to look closely at the individuals—both within and beyond the industry—who have poured into your development. By naming them, you honor their impact and begin to see the lineage of learning, resilience, and inspiration that accompanies you into every rehearsal, audition, and performance.

Take your time. Let the memories surface. Allow yourself to acknowledge the people who helped you become the artist you are becoming.

Prompt 1

What factors move you to acknowledge someone as influential in your journey?

____

____

____

Prompt 2

What qualities inspire you most in a mentor or instructor?

____

____

____

Prompt 3

Who or what drives you toward an acting career?

____

____

____

Prompt 4

How do you prefer, or intend, to thank your mentors?

Take a moment to consider the people who have supported your journey and the ways you might honor their influence.

____

____

____

Prompt 5

Do you intend to recommend your mentors to others? If so, why — and if not, why not?

Consider how your mentors have influenced your growth. Reflect honestly on whether their guidance is something you would pass forward to fellow Actors or keep to yourself.

___

___

___

Prompt 6

How might you acknowledge your mentors publicly?

Consider the ways you might honor the people who have supported your artistic journey. Will you acknowledge them through credits, social media, interviews, program notes, or simple words of gratitude shared in the right moments?

___

___

___

Prompt 7

Which form of acknowledgment feels most authentic to you?

Think about the ways you naturally express gratitude, whether through words, actions, public recognition, or quiet appreciation and choose the approach that aligns most closely with who you are as an artist.

___

___

___

Closing: Identify Your Mentors and Motivators—

As you complete this section, notice the patterns, relationships, and moments that emerge. These names and memories form a map of your artistic lineage—a reminder that your journey has never been solitary. The people you've identified represent the wisdom, encouragement, and lived experience that continue to shape your craft.

Keep this list close. Return to it when you need grounding, gratitude, or perspective. As you grow, new mentors will appear, and your understanding of past influences will deepen.

Let this record evolve with you, serving as both acknowledgement and inspiration as you continue building your artistic life.

PART II—Practical Steps to Consider

Now that you've taken time to reflect on the mentors and guides who have shaped—and continue to shape—your artistic path, it's time to move from insight into action.

This section, *Practical Steps to Consider*, invites you to take what you've uncovered throughout TRADE SECRETS and begin building the habits, tools, and systems that will support your growth as an actor. These steps are designed to help you document your journey, preserve the lessons you're learning, and strengthen the foundation of your craft as you move for-ward.

Prompt 1

Are you currently working with a journal, notebook, or book of remembrance? Are you putting it to good use?

Consider how you are documenting your progress, coaching notes, set experiences, and whether your current system supports your development effectively. Can you improve how you record these events?

____

____

____

Prompt 2

What experiences from courses, work, rehearsals, or coaching sessions have strengthened your skill set as an Actor / Artisan? How are you recording these invaluable tools and resources for future use?

Think about how your journal or notebook can preserve these lessons and serve as a lifelong training companion.

____

____

____

Prompt 3

How consistent are you in your practice?

Reflect on how often you rehearse, review material, or engage in skill-building outside of formal classes or bookings. Consider whether your current level of consistency aligns with your goals.

____

____

____

Prompt 4

Is your self-taping environment supporting your best work?

Evaluate your lighting, sound, backdrop, equipment, and overall setup. Does it reflect current industry standards? Are there small upgrades that could elevate your presentation?

____

____

____

Prompt 5

What habits or mindsets have helped—or hindered—your growth?

Identify patterns that strengthen your craft and those that may need adjustment. Consider how your attitude, discipline, and emotional resilience influence your progress.

____

____

____

Prompt 6

What practical steps can you take in the next 30 days to support your artistic development?

Think small, specific, and achievable: updating materials, scheduling practice sessions, seeking feedback, refining your tools, or revisiting foundational techniques.

____

____

____

Closing Reflection

Now that you've taken time to reflect on the mentors and guides who have shaped — and continue to shape — your artistic path, it's time to shift from insight into action.

This section, **Practical Steps to Consider**, invites you to take what you've uncovered throughout *TRADE SECRETS* and begin building the habits, tools, and systems that will support your growth as an actor. These steps are designed to help you document your journey, preserve the lessons you're learning, and strengthen the foundation of your craft as you move forward.

PART III — Beginning Your Inner Work

Before we move deeper into the work of acting, it helps to pause and understand where you are beginning. The follow-ing prompts are designed to help you center your intentions, clarify your motivations, and acknowledge what is drawing you to this craft at this moment in your life.

Each question is followed by three measured lines for your written response. Use this space to reflect honestly and without judgment. These opening reflections mark your starting point—your first moment of clarity on the page as you step into this journey.

Prompt 1

What draws you to acting right now?

Consider what is pulling you toward the craft at this moment in your life—curiosity, passion, purpose, or something still taking shape.

____

____

____

Prompt 2

Do you see acting as a career, a hobby, or something else?

Be truthful with yourself about your intentions and how you envision acting fitting into your life.

____

____

____

Prompt 3

What do you hope to discover about yourself through this book?

Think about the insights, clarity, or personal growth you hope this journey will reveal.

____

____

____

Additional Prompts to Deepen Your Inner Work

Prompt 4

What personal strengths do you believe will support you as an actor?

Reflect on qualities such as empathy, discipline, imagination, resilience, or communication.

____

____

____

Prompt 5

What fears or hesitations arise when you think about pursuing acting?

Acknowledge any doubts or internal barriers—not to judge them, but to understand them.

____

____

____

Prompt 6

How do you hope acting will impact your life beyond the craft itself?

Consider emotional growth, confidence, community, healing, or self-expression.

___

___

___

Prompt 7

What does "success" in acting mean to you personally?

Define success on your own terms, not by external expectations.

___

___

___

Closing Reflection

As you complete these opening reflections, take a moment to notice what surfaced for you. These responses form the foundation of your personal journey through this guidebook. They will evolve as you grow but capturing them now gives you a clear starting point—an anchor you can return to as your understanding deepens and your artistic path unfolds.

With this grounding in place, you're ready to move forward. The next section will guide you from inner awareness into practical steps, helping you translate reflection into action as you continue shaping your craft.

PART IV—Self-Assessment

As your reflections begin to take shape on the page, it's helpful to deepen that clarity with a more structured look at your interests and intentions. The following *Acting Interest Self-Assessment* is designed to help you identify where you are in your artistic journey and what you hope to build moving forward. Think of this section as a snapshot of your current aspirations—an honest inventory that will guide your next steps in training, exploration, and growth.

Acting Interest Self-Assessment—

Are you interested in acting as a profession, a topic of research, or a part-time resource or hobby? Before you begin this self-assessment, pause and consider what brings you to the craft at this moment. Actors come to the stage for many reasons: curiosity, passion, healing, scholarship, or the simple joy of creative expression.

Understanding your intention helps you approach the following questions with honesty. It sets the tone for how you will shape your training, your expectations, and your growth.

Motivation And Purpose

- What excites you most about acting?
  - ☐ Emotional expression
  - ☐ Fame or recognition
  - ☐ Personal growth
  - ☐ Storytelling
  - ☐ Other: ___________
- What do you hope to gain from acting?
  - ☐ A career
  - ☐ A creative outlet
  - ☐ A deeper understanding of human behavior
  - ☐ Other: ___________

9. Professional Aspirations
   - Would you consider formal training (e.g., acting school, workshops)?
     - ☐ Yes
     - ☐ No
     - ☐ Maybe

- What type of acting interests you most?
  - ☐ Commercials
  - ☐ Film
  - ☐ Television
  - ☐ Theater
  - ☐ Voice acting
  - ☐ Other: ___________
- Are you open to relocating for acting opportunities?
  - ☐ Yes
  - ☐ No
  - ☐ Maybe

10. Research and Academic Interests
    - Are you studying acting as part of a research project?
      - ☐ Yes
      - ☐ No
    - What aspect of acting are you researching?
      - ☐ Cultural comparisons
      - ☐ History
      - ☐ Psychological impact
      - ☐ Techniques
      - ☐ Other: ___________
11. Part-Time or Hobbyist Engagement
    - Have you participated in any casual acting activities?
      - ☐ Community theater
      - ☐ Improv groups
      - ☐ Online skits
      - ☐ None yet
    - How much time can you dedicate to acting weekly?
      - ☐ Less than 2 hours
      - ☐ 2–5 hours

- ☐ 5+ hours

- What kind of environment do you prefer?
  - ☐ Collaborative and social
  - ☐ Low-pressure and exploratory
  - ☐ Structured and goal-oriented

12. Experience and Skill Level

- Have you acted before?
  - ☐ Yes, professionally
  - ☐ Yes, informally
  - ☐ No
- Which genres or roles appeal to you most?
  - ☐ Comedy
  - ☐ Drama
  - ☐ Fantasy/Sci-fi
  - ☐ Realistic/Documentary
  - ☐ Other: ____________
- Which skills do you feel confident in?
  - ☐ Emotional range
  - ☐ Improvisation
  - ☐ Live performance
  - ☐ Memorization
  - ☐ Other: ____________

14. Support and Resources

- Do you have access to acting mentors or communities?
  - ☐ Yes
  - ☐ No
  - ☐ Looking for one
- Are you familiar with audition processes?
  - ☐ Yes
  - ☐ No

- ☐ Somewhat

- What resources have you explored?

  - ☐ Acting apps
  - ☐ Books
  - ☐ Online courses
  - ☐ Workshops
  - ☐ Other: ___________

CLOSING REFLECTION

As you complete this self-assessment and look over your responses you will notice patterns emerge. These responses offer a clear snapshot of where you stand today and what your motivations are, where your interests lie, and the possibilities you are beginning to identify with and/or intend to explore.

There is no right or wrong place to begin; what matters is your willingness to understand yourself as an artist. Carry this clarity with you as you move into the next section, where your intentions will start to take shape through practice, reflection, and guided development.

PART V—Transition Into Acting Focus

With a clearer understanding of your motivations and the role acting may play in your life, you are now ready to refine your direction with greater intention.

The section, **Transition Into Acting Focus**, invites you to look more closely at the specific areas that draw your interest—artistic, practical, or personal. This is where your aspirations begin to take shape, helping you identify the path that aligns most naturally with your goals, your lifestyle, and your evolving sense of self as an actor.

Focus and Direction

Now that you have explored your initial interests and motivators, this section invites you to consider where you want to direct your energy. Whether you are pursuing acting as a career, a creative outlet, an academic inquiry, or a part-time passion, clarifying your focus helps you make choices that support your goals, your lifestyle, and your personal growth.

Use the following categories to identify what matters most to you at this stage of your journey.

1. Career vs. Hobby

- ☐ I want to act as a full-time career
- ☐ I want to act as a part-time pursuit
- ☐ I want to act as a casual hobby
- ☐ I am undecided but exploring options

2. Artistic Direction

- ☐ Film acting (movies, short films)
- ☐ Improv or experimental performance
- ☐ Stage acting (theater, live performance)
- ☐ Television acting (series, commercials)
- ☐ Voice acting (animation, audiobooks, games)

3. Skill Development

- ☐ Character building and role study
- ☐ Emotional range and expression
- ☐ Improvisation and spontaneity
- ☐ Memorization and script work
- ☐ Physical presence and movement
- ☐ Other: ____________________

4. Personal Growth

- ☐ Building confidence
- ☐ Connecting with others
- ☐ Expanding cultural or psychological understanding

- ☐ Exploring self-expression
- ☐ Storytelling and creativity
- ☐ Other: ____________________

5. **Practical Considerations**
   - ☐ Comfortable with rehearsal schedules
   - ☐ Need balance with other responsibilities
   - ☐ Open to relocation or travel for roles
   - ☐ Prefer local/community opportunities
   - ☐ Willing to audition regularly
   - ☐ Other: ____________________

6. **Support and Resources**
   - ☐ I belong to an acting community or group
   - ☐ I have mentors or acting coaches
   - ☐ I understand audition processes
   - ☐ I am seeking more resources before committing
   - ☐ I have explored books, courses, and workshops
   - ☐ Other: ____________________

Closing Reflection

As you complete this section, take a moment to sit with the clarity you've uncovered. The choices you've made here reveal where your artistic energy is naturally gathering—whether in the realm of craft, career, creativity, or personal expression. These insights are not fixed; they are living indicators of what matters to you right now.

What's most important is that your focus reflects your truth. Let this understanding guide the decisions you make next: the training you pursue, the opportunities you welcome, and the way you show up for your work. With this foundation in place, you are stepping forward with intention, aligned with the path that best supports your growth as an actor.

PART VI—Knowledge About the Craft

Before moving deeper into training, it's helpful to pause and take stock of what you already understand about the craft. Every actor begins from a different place—some with formal study, some with casual exposure, and others with only curiosity. Recognizing your current level of awareness helps you approach work ahead with honesty and intention.

This next section, ***Do You Know Anything About Act-ing?***, invites you to explore your existing understanding of performance, technique, and industry. By identifying what you already know, you gain a clearer sense of your starting point and the areas where you may want to grow.

Do You Know Anything About Acting?

Acting is both an art and a craft, requiring imagination, discipline, and an awareness of performance techniques. Before stepping into auditions, rehearsals, or even casual stage play, it's important to reflect on your exposure to acting, your familiarity with various methods, and you understand-ing of the industry.

By exploring these questions, you identify your foundation, uncover areas for development, and begin shaping how you want to approach learning and practicing the craft. Acting begins with awareness—of the work, the industry, and yourself.

This section helps you reflect on what you already know, from personal experiences to professional insights—so you can understand where you are now and prepare for where you intend to go. Use the following questions to identify what this stage of your journey reveals about your current understanding of acting.

1. General Awareness

- ☐ I can describe what acting means to me
- ☐ I know the difference between stage and screen acting
- ☐ I've thought about how Actors prepare for roles

2. **Personal Exposure**
   - ☐ I have no prior acting experience
   - ☐ I have participated in a play, skit, or performance
   - ☐ I have done informal acting (school, community theater, improv)
   - ☐ I have studied or read about acting methods (e.g., Stanislavski, Method Acting)
3. **Knowledge of the Profession**
   - ☐ I do not know much about the professional side of acting
   - ☐ I know about training options (acting schools, workshops, online courses)
   - ☐ I understand the audition process
   - ☐ I am aware of what Agents, Directors, and producers look for in Actors
4. **Skills and Techniques**
   - ☐ I know techniques for memorizing scripts
   - ☐ I understand improvisation in acting
   - ☐ I am familiar with emotional range and character building
   - ☐ I am not familiar with acting techniques
   - ☐ I have heard of voice projection and stage presence
5. **Industry and Culture**
   - ☐ I do not know much about the industry
   - ☐ I know the difference between commercial, film, theater, and voice acting
   - ☐ I understand how Actors build careers (networking, portfolios, showreels)
   - ☐ I am aware of challenges Actors face (competition, rejection, long hours)
6. **Self-Reflection**
   - ☐ I feel confident performing in front of others

- ☐ I know what types of roles or genres appeal to me
- ☐ I understand my motivation for exploring acting (career, research, hobby)
- ☐ I am still figuring out my interest in acting

7. **Why I Chose These Skills**
   - ☐ What made these skills stand out to you as priorities?
   - ☐ How do these skills connect to your long-term goals in acting?
   - ☐ Which experiences (positive or challenging) influenced your choices?
   - ☐ Do these skills reflect strengths you want to refine or gaps you want to close?

8. What drew you to these areas? What do you hope they will unlock for you?
   - ☐ What personal curiosity, passion, or need led you to these areas?
   - ☐ How do you imagine these skills expanding your creative range?
   - ☐ What opportunities do you hope these skills will open for you?
   - ☐ How will strengthening these areas support your confidence or artistic identity?

9. **Steps I Will Take To Strengthen These Skills**
   - ☐ What specific actions will you take to develop each skill?
   - ☐ Which habits or routines will support consistent practice?
   - ☐ What obstacles might you face, and how will you navigate them?
   - ☐ Who can support or mentor you as you grow in these areas?

10. **List classes, coaches, resources, or practice habits you plan to pursue.**
    - ☐ Which classes or workshops align with your goals?
    - ☐ Are there coaches or mentors you want to work with?
    - ☐ What books, apps, or online platforms will you use?
    - ☐ What self-directed exercises or daily practices will you commit to?
11. Timeline for Growth
    - ☐ What is your starting point — when will you begin?
    - ☐ How long will you focus on each skill or phase of development?
    - ☐ What milestones will help you stay on track?
    - ☐ How will you adjust your timeline if your goals evolve?
12. When will you begin? How will you measure progress?
    - ☐ What date or timeframe marks your official start?
    - ☐ What indicators will show you're improving (feedback, performance quality, comfort level)?
    - ☐ How often will you check in with yourself to assess progress?
    - ☐ What will "success" look like for you at the end of this period?

Closing Reflection

As you finish this section, take a moment to acknowledge the knowledge and experiences you already carry with you. Whether your familiarity with acting is extensive, limited, or somewhere in between, this honest assessment gives you a clear understanding of where you are beginning.

Every actor starts from a different place, and what mat-ters most is your willingness to learn, explore, and grow. Let these insights guide you as you move forward, helping you approach the craft with awareness, curiosity, and a deeper understanding of the path you are shaping for yourself.

PART VII—Acting Approach Transition

As you begin shaping your path as an actor, it is helpful to understand not only what interests you, but how you naturally learn, grow, and engage with the craft. Every actor develops their skills differently. Some through structured training and others through experimentation, observation, or hands on practice.

The *Acting Approach* section invites you to explore your personal learning style, the methods that resonate with you, and the kind of training environment where you feel most supported. Your responses will help you identify the approach that aligns with your strengths, your goals, and the way you want to experience the art of acting.

Acting Approach—

Acting is a doorway into imagination—a chance to step into new worlds, embody different lives, and discover hidden parts of yourself. Whether you dream of the stage lights, the camera's gaze, or simply the joy of storytelling, the way you choose to learn acting will shape your journey. This questionnaire invites you to pause and reflect:

- What excites you most?
- How do you want to grow?
- Where will your first steps take you?

Your answers will help illuminate the path toward your own unique performance adventure.

Every actor's path is unique. Use this checklist to explore what you already know, what excites you, and how you want to grow as you begin learning to act.

1. Learning Style

☐ I learn best through improvisation and experimentation

☐ I learn best through observation and imitation

☐ I learn best through practice and repetition

- ☐ I prefer self-guided study (books, videos, online resources)
- ☐ I prefer structured classes with clear guidance
- ☐ I prefer workshops or short-term intensives

2. Training Methods

- ☐ I want to attend a formal acting school or academy
- ☐ I want to combine multiple methods for a balanced approach
- ☐ I want to explore online courses or tutorials
- ☐ I want to join community theater or local acting groups
- ☐ I want to study specific acting techniques (Stanislavski, Method Acting, Meisner, etc.)

3. Practical Experience

- ☐ I prefer to build skills before auditioning
- ☐ I want to audition early to gain experience
- ☐ I want to begin with small roles in local productions
- ☐ I want to join improv groups or acting clubs
- ☐ I want to practice casually with friends or peers

4. Personal Goals

- ☐ I want to act as a hobby or personal enrichment
- ☐ I want to act as part of academic or research interest
- ☐ I want to act to open professional opportunities
- ☐ I want to build confidence in public speaking and performance
- ☐ I want to develop storytelling skills
- ☐ I want to explore self-expression and creativity

5. Commitment and Resources

- ☐ I can dedicate less than 2 hours per week
- ☐ I can dedicate 2–5 hours per week
- ☐ I can dedicate 5+ hours per week

- ☐ I am willing to invest financially in training / workshops
- ☐ I have access to mentors or acting communities
- ☐ I need to seek more resources before committing

6. Self-Reflection

- ☐ I anticipate challenges like stage fright or memorization
- ☐ I bring strengths such as voice, creativity, or presence
- ☐ I want to measure progress through feedback and performance opportunities
- ☐ I want to measure progress through personal growth and confidence

As you complete this section, take a moment to notice the preferences and patterns that emerged. These choices reveal how you learn best, what inspires you, and where you may want to focus on your early training.

There is no single path to becoming an actor, the one that fits your rhythm, your curiosity, and your capacity for growth.

Let these insights guide your next steps as you continue building a foundation that supports your unique artistic journey.

Closing Reflection

You have now explored your motivations, interests, knowledge, and personal approach to the craft of acting. Each section in this chapter has invited you to look inward to con-sider what draws you to performance, how you learn best, where your strengths lie, and what you hope to build as you move forward. These reflections form the early architecture of your artistic identity. They reveal not only where you are beginning, but also the possibilities that lie ahead.

As you move beyond this chapter, carry these insights with you. They will serve as a compass as you encounter new techniques, new challenges, and new opportunities.

Acting is a journey shaped by curiosity, discipline, and self-awareness. By taking the time to understand your start-ing point, you have already taken your first meaningful step into the craft.

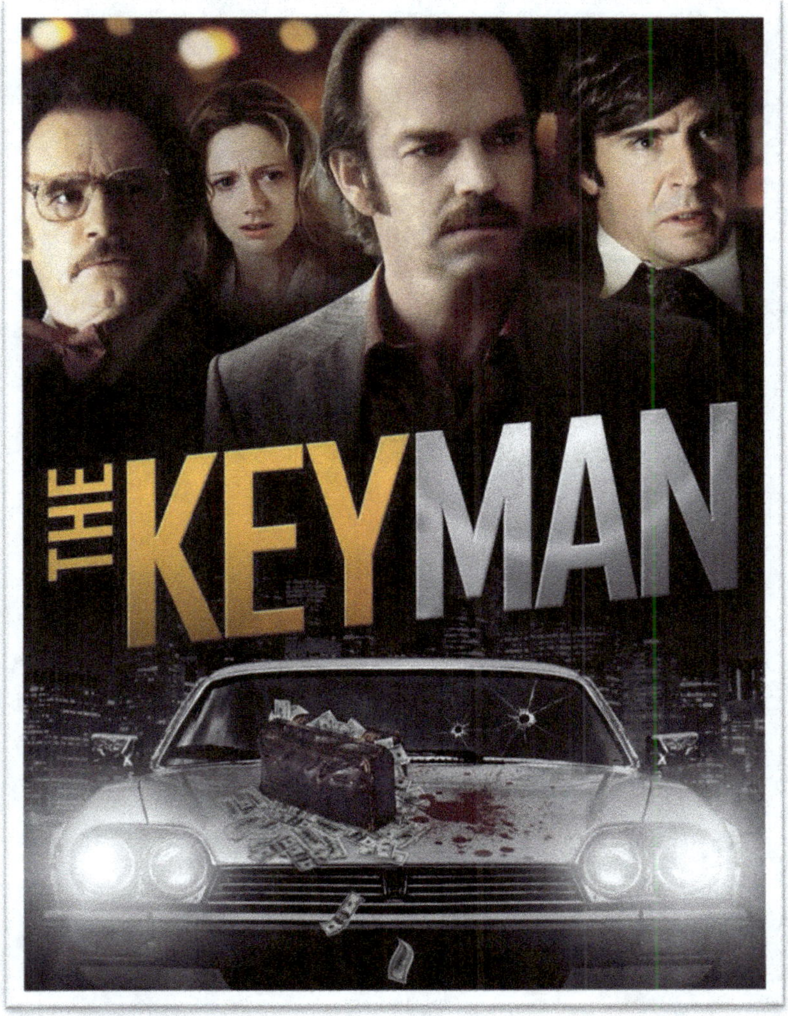

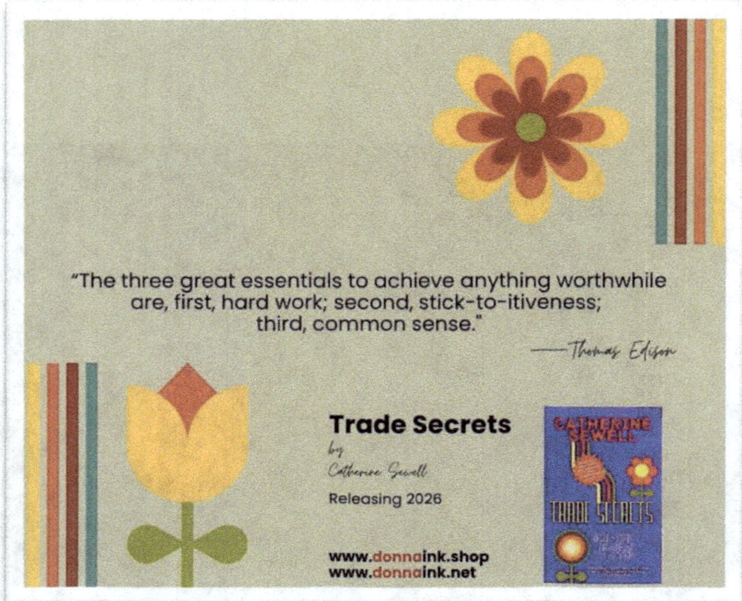
"The three great essentials to achieve anything worthwhile are, first, hard work; second, stick-to-itiveness; third, common sense."
—Thomas Edison
Trade Secrets
by
Catherine Sewell
Releasing 2026
www.donnaink.shop
www.donnaink.net
CATHERINE SEWELL
TRADE SECRETS

"Nearly every man who develops an idea works it up to the point where it looks impossible, and then he gets discouraged. That's not the place to become discouraged."
—Thomas Edison
Trade Secrets
by
Catherine Sewell
Releasing 2026
www.donnaink.shop
www.donnaink.net
CATHERINE SEWELL
TRADE SECRETS

ABOUT THE AUTHOR

CATHERINE SEWELL
WHERE LIVED EXPERIENCE MEETS AUTHENTIC PERFORMANCE

AN AWARD-WINNING ARTIST

For more than two decades, Catherine Rogers Sewell has built a dynamic and multifaceted career in the entertainment industry, spanning film, television, commercials, and voiceover work. Her creative range extends behind the camera as well; alongside her co-producer, she earned the *NC Society of Historians'* prestigious *Paul Green Multi-Media Award* for their documentary *The House in the Horseshoe.*

In 2004, Catherine achieved her *Screen Actors Guild (SAG)* eligibility through her memorable portrayal of Mrs. Newman—the iconic "nosey neighbor, "in a nationwide *Travelocity Commercial* campaign.

Rooted in a rich tapestry of life experience as a mother, grandmother, teacher, psychologist, and college professor, Catherine brings authenticity and emotional truth to every *real people* performance she delivers. Outside of her on camera work, she enjoys reading nonfiction, writing, gardening, and nurturing her artistic spirit through jazz singing and live performance.

SUMMER CATCH

VISIT THE AUTHOR

SOCIAL MEDIA & WEBSITES

Here are my links to social media, websites, and more.

SOCIAL MEDIA

Facebook:

https://www.facebook.com/catherine.sewell3
https://www.facebook.com/donnainkpublications

Instagram:

https://www.instagram.com/actingtrainercatherinesewell
https://www.instagram.com/donnainkpublications

LinkedIn:

https://www.linkedin.com/in/catherine-sewell-869300251
https://www.linkedin.com/in/donnaink

Pinterest:

https://www.pinterest.com/DonnaInkPublications

Tumblr:

https://www.tumblr.com/DonnaInk

YouTube:

https://www.youtube.com/donnainkpublications

WEBSITES

Catherine Sewell:
https://catherinesewell.wixsite.com/actress

Catherine Sewell on IMDb:
https://www.imdb.com/name/nm1423080

DonnaInk Publications:
Catherine Sewell ~ Actress, Author, Filmmaker
https://www.donnaink.net/catherinesewell

CATHERINE'S CREDITS

ACTOR, AUTHOR, FILMMAKER, PRODUCER

Fast Lane Talent Agency
(980) 224-0337
fastlanetalent@gmail.com

CATHERINE SEWELL - SAG-AFTRA

Résumé

COMMERCIAL		
Food Lion (SAG)	Featured (Food Receipient)	GSD&M Idea City LLC
Legacy at North Augusta	Principal (Resident)	Legacy at North Augusta Media
Rutherford Tourism	Principal (Older Wife)	Apple Box Cinema Company
Nascar 2018	Featured (Receptionist)	GLP Creative
Boosterthon 2017 "Teacher's Meeting"	Principal (Mrs. Clark)	Booster Enterprises, Inc.
Travelocity	Principal Speaking (Nosey Neighbor)	Mr. Big Films, Inc. (Chicago)
Copies Plus	Principal Speaking(Copier Operator)	Time Warner Cable Adcast
Smith-Stokes Car Dealerships	Principal Speaking (Granny)	Westokes Advertising
The Chiropractic Center of Pembroke	Principal Speaking (Patient)	Time Warner Cable Adcast
First Comfort Heating & Cooling	Principal Speaking (Customer)	Tellurvision Video Production
The Gathering Storm (Book Trailer)	Seance Participant	Run and Gun Films

FILM (Full List upon request)		
Delmo Berry (2024)	(Lead)	Koontz Films
The Christy Martin Biopic	Background (Spectator)	Anonymous Content, etc. produc
Billy Two Rivers	(Lead)	Koontz Films

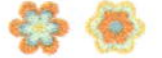

Jailhouse Wedding (2019)	(Supporting) Deputy Laura King	Perry Ball Productions
Darlin' (2018)	(Dayplayer) Mrs. Freeman	Little Biter LLC/P McIntosh
Tom Destry	(lead) Norror	Koontz Films
Cooper Sky	(Lead) Norror	Koontz Films
Fever Dreams-It's My House	(Supporting Lead) May Downing	Feedback Films
A Lovely Sunrise	(Supporting) Mandy	Tar Heel Cinema
Elbow Grease	(Supporting) Granny Blythe	Elbow Grease/Flat World Prod.
Tobaccoland:Before	(Supporting) Louanne Royal	Forrest Entertainment, NYC
Junebug	(Lead) Aunt Mable	Continuous Take Productions
Will to Power	(Supporting) Mrs. Ryter/Patient	Omega Films/ Los Angeles
Off-Ramp to Eden	(Supporting) Bernice	Blindside Illumination Product
Praise Band	(Principal) Choir Lady 1	Dir. David Moody/Elevating Ent
Left in the Ditch	(Supporting) Aimee	Dir.Joseph Gerbino, NYU
Foresight	(Supporting) Mrs. Fuller/Psychic	Daytype Films, NC
Cowboy Trails	(Supporting) Stella the Storekeeper	Circle M Productions, NC
QVC	(Lead) Gretta	Dir. Jesse Pikes/ NCSA
Louie the Moon	(Principal) Grandma Guzzi	Pretend Productions, NC
Clean Up on Aisle Five	(Supporting) Elderly Woman	Circus Dogs Productions
Britney's Summer in Paris	(Supporting) Wife	Lodger Productions
Haunted Mind	(Supporting) Mother	Dir. Ted Ferris/UNCSA
Clay	(Supporting) Lorraine/Mother	Dir. Brad Baker/UNCSA

The Devil's Game

STAND-IN/BODY DOUBLE (FILM)

Main Street	(Stand-in/Body Double)Ellen Burstyn	Main Street Productions
The Key Man	(Stand-in) Hugo Weaving & Judy Greer	Keyman Productions
Divine Secrets of the Ya Ya Sisterhood	(Stand-in) Dame Maggie Smith	Sisterhood Productions/WB

Divine Secrets of the Ya Ya Sisterhood

TELEVISION - EPISODIC

It's Supernatural w Sid Roth (2020)	Ryan Johnson's Mother	New Day Pictures International
Homicide for the Holidays-Season 3 Ep. 303 (2020)	Elaine Denney	Jupiter Entertainment/Oxygen
Famous and Afraid (2019)	Old Woman Farmer Ghost	Jupiter Entertainment/Travel C
Mark of a Killer (2019)	Leafie Mason	Jupiter Entertainment/ Oxygen
It's Supernatural w Sid Roth (2018)	Principal (Woman)	New Day Pictures International
Killer Couples Ep. 10:03 (2018)	Principal (Etta Jean Westbrook - Victim)	ID/Jupiter Entertainment
Homicide Hunter Ep. 703 "Raise the Dead"	Principal (Ann Ives)	ID/Jupiter Entertainment
Losing My Soul	Supporting (Scarlett)	Envy Rue
"Days That Shook the World" (Pearl Harbor)	Co-star (Head Nurse)	BBC / Lion TV
Happily Never After-Ep307 (2014)	Lead (Lou Patton)	Investigative Discovery/M2Pict
It's Supernatural with Sid Roth	Principal (Frances Medcalf)	New Day Pictures International
Inspiration Today-"Heaven" Series with Trudy Harris	Principal (Billie Patterson)	INSP Network
Cool Carolina Nights Soap Drama	Principal (Dorothy Bennett)	JBG Media Productions/Atlanta
Southern Fried Stings	Dayplayer (Ella) Wife	TruTV/ Zoo Productions
Rusty Bucket Kids Show	Recurring (Mary Sue Ellen)	Studio in the Woods
"NC Wanted"(Linda Meeker Story)	Co-star (Linda's Mother)	Fox 50 /WRAZ
"Psychic Detectives" (Lost in Transit-Pat McCormick)	Title Lead (Pat McCormick)	Court TV / Story House Product

"All You Can Eat"

LIVE HOSTING

Screen Actors Guild 75th Anniversary Gala

INDUSTRIAL/CORPORATE/VIDEO

Aspen Dental (2022)	Lead-Patient	Aspen Dental Clinics
Georgia Power Heroes (2020)	Heart Attack Victim's Wife	GDI Productions /Georgia
Above & Beyond (2019)	Grandma	Passion City Church /Georgia
Cigarette Warning Ad Print	Smoker	RTI International
Grief Share "Surviving the Holidays"	Wife	Church Initiative/Sam Hodges

Nat. Institute of Health "Communicating Effectively"	Principal (Nurse)	Dir. K.Cullen, Emot. Creatures
Divorce Care	Wife	Church Initiative/Sam Hodges
US Treasury Depart, IRS	Principal (Receptionist)	Encore Video Productions
TheraSim Medical Video	Lead (Patient)	Jean-Paul Dame, Producer
Renal Failure Industrial	Lead (Patient)	Back Focus Films
Coldwell Banker United Reality	Lead (Home Buyer)	Brown Studies
Alzheimer's Association	Principal (Caretaker Student)	Horizon Video
Failure Free Reading	Lead (Interviewer)	Digital Images
GlaxoSmithKline	Featured(Receptionist & Casino Player)	Horizon Video
Standarized Patient Program	Standarized Patient	UNC Med School Clinical Skills

Standarized Patient Program

BROADCAST TV		
Live at Nine (Talk Show)	Co-Host (1998-2010)	WBF-TV Channel 46
Cooking Show Special Edition	Host	WBF-TV Channel 46
Blank Surfaces	Host	Across the Canvas Productions
The Lee County Fair	Co-Host (4-years)	WBF-TV Channel 46
Elections Primary 2000	Co-Anchor	WBF-TV Channel 46
Insight North Carolina	Correspondent (2002-2004)	Eno River Media Productions

The Local Scene

VOICE OVER/RADIO HOST		
Don't Fear the Reeper Audio Plays	Narrator and Valerie	Shadowdog Productions
Scotia Village Ms. NC Senior Pageant	Voice-Over	Life 103 FM
89.1 FM	Voice-Over	89.1 FM in Australia
KAK Radio	Voice-Over	KAK Radio Kentucky
93.7 FM WYAH	Voice-Over	93.7 FM WYAH Winchester, Kentu
TANF Project in Louisiana	Narration	Simple Machines Prod. for Uni.
G105	Pearl (Weather-comedic spot)	G105 Raleigh, NC
For Your Health Series	Host	WDSG 107.9 FM
Around Town with Cathy Sewell	Host	WDSG 107.9 FM

Stanley Western Auto Home Center	Voice-Over	WDSG 107.9 FM
Southern Jewelers	Voice-Over	WDSG 107.9 FM
McNeil Paint and Decorating Center	Voice-Over	WDSG 107.9 FM
Lee Builder Mart	Voice-Over	WDSG 107.9 FM
Myres Animal Hospital (2 spots)	Voice-Over	WDSG 107.9 FM
Computerized Tax Services	Voice-Over	WDSG 107.9 FM
Jo Ann's Fashions	Voice-Over	WDSG 107.9 FM

WDSG 107.9 FM

THEATER		
Footloose (2017)	Adult Ensemble	Temple Theatre
His Wonderful Presence: Here and Now	Charlotte/ 18 Years	Mary Ann Sadler
Bark	Beth Ann	Grace Ellis
By Noon	Mrs. Parker	7 AM Productions

Footlight Players

MUSIC VIDEO		
Madonna Nash (2011)	Lead (Bernice)	Shutter Blade Productions
It's Supernatural	Featured (Widow)	New Day Pictures International

Roxanna Demers

TRAINING		
College Drama	Theater/Acting	Anderson University
Through the Eyes of Casting	Jen Inguli	
Audition Techniques	Tim Ross	
Acting for the Camera	Tracy Kilpatrick	
Acting for the Camera	Amy Jo Berman	
Acting for the Camera	Richard Futch, Bob Luke & Jordan Beswick	Tom Logan & Tom Webb
Commercial Techniques	Corrigan & Johnston & Elyse Williams	JD Lewis & Timothy O'Keefe
Voice and Diction	Susan S. Stewart & Jay O'Berski	Rick Azar & Dalton Thomas
Accent Reduction/Diction	Rick Caballada Azar	
Voice-Over	Rowell Howell & John Demers	
Vocal Voice (Singer)	Marilyn Turner & Denise Robinette	Joan Le Tourneau

Catherine has over 18-years of experience in film, television, commercials, print, and voice-over work. Her life experiences as a mother, grandmother, teacher, psychologist, college professor and administrator help her deliver strong "real people" performances.

Physical Characteristics / Measurements

Height: 5'4" Weight: 124 lbs

Business Woman, Drive Standard Shift, Good with animals, Good with children, Handgun training, Retailer, School Administrator, Shoot firearms, Storyteller, Teacher, Teleprompter, Trained psychologist, Aerobics, Archery, Badminton, Bowling, Cycling, Equestrian - General, Equestrian - Western, Fishing, Ice Skating, Jump Rope, Ping Pong, Roller Skating, Running - General, Shooting - Revolver/Automatic, Shooting - Rifle, Snow Skiing - General, Softball, Swimming - ability - general, Swimming - breast stroke, Swimming - butterfly, Swimming - diving, Swimming - freestyle, Tennis, Volleyball, Water Skiing, Audio Prompter, Dance Ballroom, Dance Line/Country, Dance Swing, Dancer, Ear Prompter, Firearms, Harmonica, Host, Improvisation, Licensed Driver, Modeling, Percussion, Piano, Precision Driver, Singer, Teleprompter, Vocal Range: Mezzo Soprano, Voiceover, American - Southern Accent, British - BBC English Accent, British - Cockney Accent, Spanish Accent

This is a non-comprehensive list of Catherine Sewell's total credited work, which has continued since undertaking of this book project.

What is recorded here is her standard list of works shared online; a more comprehensive list continues to be developed.

MERCHANDISE

CATHERINE SEWELL & TRADE SECRETS

CATHERINE SEWELL
TRADE SECRETS
REAL-TIME ROADMAP TO ACTING
Trade Secrets
dpInk

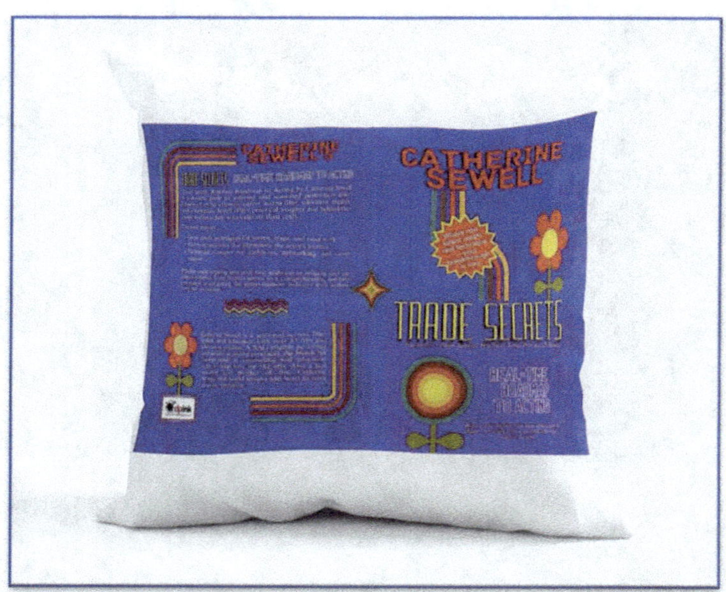
CATHERINE SEWELL
TRADE SECRETS
REAL-TIME ROADMAP TO ACTING

A
K
Q
CATHERINE SEWELL
TRADE SECRETS
REAL-TIME ROADMAP TO ACTING

CATHERINE SEWELL'S
TRADE SECRETS
CATHERINE SEWELL
TRADE SECRETS
REAL-TIME ROADMAP TO ACTING
dplink

CATHERINE SEWELL
TRADE SECRETS
ATHERINE SEWEL

TRADE SECRETS
www.catherinesewell.com

TRADE SECRETS
Catherine Sewell
www.catherinesewell.com

BIBLIOGRAPHY

RESOURCES IDENTIFIED IN TRADE SECRETS

#	Source Type	Correct Chicago Citation
1	Book	Brandon, Mark. *Winning Auditions: 101 Strategies for Actors*. New York: Limelight Editions, 2005.
2	Website	Casablancas, John. "What Are Industrial Films?" *John Casablancas*. November 26, 2012. https://www.jcasablancas.com/what-are-industrial-films/..
3	Online News Article	Kekatos, Mary. "COVID-19 Timeline: How the Deadly Virus and the World's Response Have Evolved over 4 Years." *ABC News*. March 11, 2024. https://abcnews.go.com/..

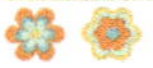

EXCLUSIVE
Entertainment
EXCLUSIVE
A FILM WRITTEN & DIRECTED BY
POLLYANNA MCINTOSH
Darlin'
Don't mess with mother's nature.
SXSW 2019
FILM FESTIVAL

ABOUT THE PUBLISHER

DONNAINK PUBLICATIONS

"Where voices rise, genres converge, and legacies are born."

DonnaInk Publications is a woman owned boutique publishing house founded by strategist and author Donna L. Quesinberry. Rooted in cross genre innovation and author empowerment, DonnaInk champions diverse voices, unconventional narratives, and legacy driven storytelling. The press blends editorial precision with creative vision, offering authors a collaborative environment from concept to completion.

Production And Creative Services

- Author platform development and media integration
- Book design (cover, spine, back, interior layout)
- Cross-platform publishing (TV, podcast, web media tie ins)
- Distribution setup for retail, wholesale, and global markets
- Editorial development and manuscript evaluation
- Event collateral and branded merchandise
- Ghostwriting and author coaching
- Imprint branding and genre alignment
- ISBN assignment and Library of Congress registration

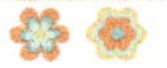

- Print and digital publishing across trade, academic, and creative formats
- Promotional asset creation (flyers, banners, press kits)
- Series development, legacy packaging, and strategic branding support

A Multi Imprint Creative Ecosystem

DonnaInk curates a dynamic catalog spanning poetry, political thrillers, memoirs, metaphysical works, and cultural non-fiction. Its specialized imprints—including 2nd Spirit Books, Beat Deep Books, Creations by Q For You!, Faces of Rap Mothers, Ironmantle Books, Katsujinken, Laughingcleaver Press, Little Buggy Productions, Moondust Media, Nocturnum's Muse, Owlhouse, Pashar Sage Press, and Thunderforge Pubs, amplify distinct genres and communities while upholding a shared commitment to authenticity and craft.

More than a publisher, DonnaInk is a creative ecosystem. Authors receive hands on editorial guidance, strategic brand development, and access to multimedia platforms that elevate their work beyond the page. With global reach and boutique precision, DonnaInk transforms manuscripts into movements.

For more information, visit: www.donnaink.net
Email: msdonnalquesinberry@donnaink.net
Text: (301) 888 2414

ABOUT THE IMPRINT

OWLHOUSE

"Where quiet truths meet powerful storytelling."

OwlHouse is a contemplative, craft-driven imprint of DonnaInk Publications dedicated to publishing works that illuminate the inner landscapes of thought, imagination, and human experience. From literary fiction and reflective nonfiction to poetry, folklore, and philosophical explorations, OwlHouse curates titles that invite readers into deeper seeing, deeper feeling, and deeper understanding.

This imprint thrives at the intersection of intellect and intuittion—where story meets symbolism, where quiet truths meet bold ideas, and where narrative becomes a lantern for the mind. Whether revealing the subtle architecture of the human spirit or spotlighting emerging voices in literary arts, OwlHouse delivers resonant works that linger long after the final page.

With a focus on author development and thoughtful curation, OwlHouse supports contributors through editorial refinement, conceptual framing, and brand positioning. Many titles extend into companion experiences—readers' guides, reflective journals, workshops, and literary salons—making OwlHouse a haven for writers and thinkers who want their work to enlighten, inspire, and endure.

From moonlit musings to fireside philosophies, OwlHouse is where insight gathers, imagination roams, and time-less literature finds its home.

For more information, visit: www.donnaink.net
Email: msdonnalquesinberry@donnaink.net
Text: (301) 888-2414

ABOUT THE IMPRINT

BEAT DEEP BOOKS

"Where creatives speak, stars shine, and stories perform."

Beat Deep Books is a media forward imprint of DonnaInk Publications dedicated to publishing and promoting voices from the entertainment, arts, and creative industries. From filmmakers and musicians to actors, authors, and cultural influencers, Beat Deep Books curates content that reflects the rhythm of modern storytelling and the heartbeat of global artistry.

This imprint thrives at the intersection of literature and lifestyle—where memoir meets music, poetry meets performance, and narrative meets notoriety. Whether capturing the behind-the-scenes grit of celebrity life or spotlighting emerging creatives in film, fashion, and stage, Beat Deep Books delivers high impact works that resonate across platforms.

With a focus on cross industry collaboration, Beat Deep supports contributors through editorial development, brand strategy, and multimedia exposure. Titles often extend into companion media—documentaries, podcasts, digital shorts, and live events—making Beat Deep a launchpad for creatives who want their stories to move, speak, and shine.

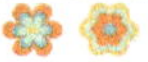

From red carpets to recording booths, Beat Deep Books is where culture performs, and legacy begins.

For more information, visit: www.donnaink.net
Email: msdonnalquesinberry@donnaink.net
Text: (301) 888 2414

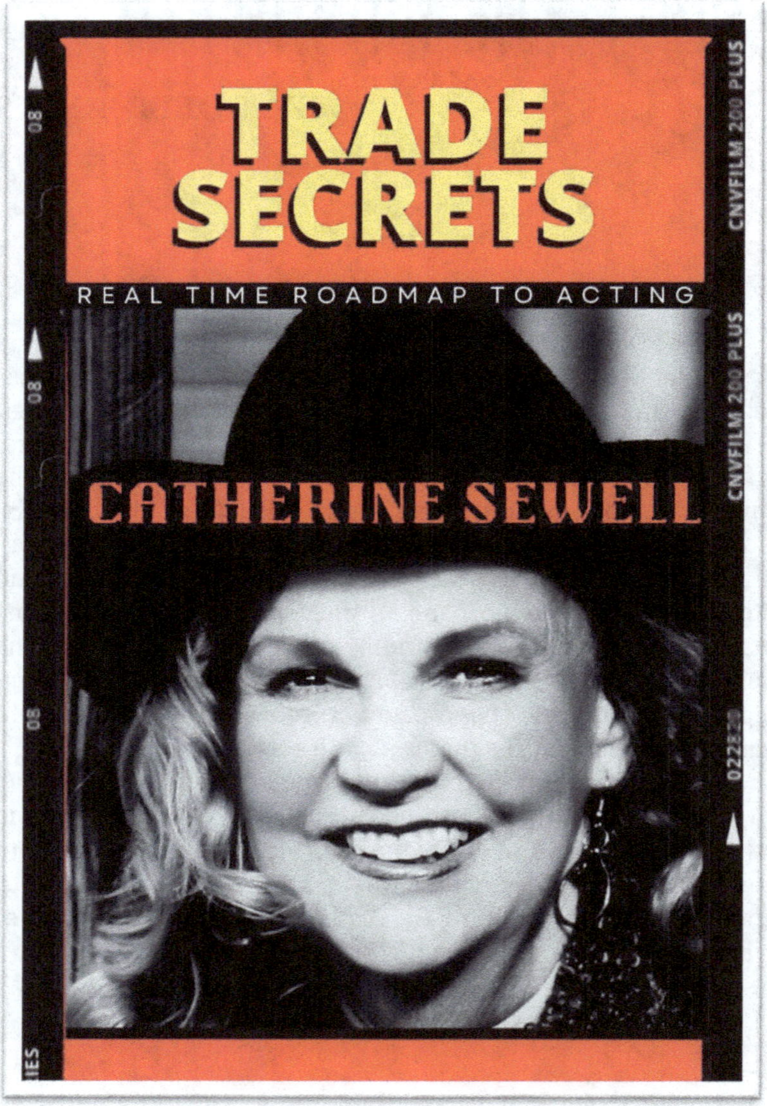
TRADE SECRETS
REAL TIME ROADMAP TO ACTING
CATHERINE SEWELL
CNVFILM 200 PLUS
CNVFILM 200 PLUS

APPENDIX A

EMERGING ACTORS REGIONAL "HUB" DIRECTORY

This list focuses on **regional casting, training, and production-community resources** that emerging actors actually use derived from U.S. hubs outside of state film commissions.

ATLANTA (SOUTHEAST HUB)

- **800 Casting** — https://www.800casting.com
- **Houghton Talent** (regional agency) — https://www.houghtontalent.com
- **The People Store** — https://www.peoplestore.net
- **Get Scene Studios** (training) — https://www.getscenestudios.com

DMV (DC–MARYLAND–VIRGINIA)

- **Stonehenge Casting** — https://www.teamstonehenge.com
- **DC Actors for Hire** — https://www.dcactors.org
- **Studio Acting Conservatory** — https://www.studioacting.org

- WIFV DC (Women in Film & Video) — https://www.wifv.org

NEW YORK CITY

- **Actors Connection** — https://www.actorsconnection.com
- **One on One / Next Level** — https://www.oneononenyc.com
- **Backstage NYC** — https://www.backstage.com
- **The Barrow Group** (training) — https://www.barrowgroup.org

LOS ANGELES

- **Casting Frontier** — https://www.castingfrontier.com
- **LA Casting (via Casting Networks)** — https://www.castingnetworks.com
- **The Groundlings** — https://www.groundlings.com
- **Margie Haber Studio** — https://margiehaber.com

CHICAGO

- **Second City** — https://www.secondcity.com
- **Chicago Acting in Film Meetup (CAFM)** — https://www.chicagoactinginfilm.org
- **Paskal Rudnicke Casting** — https://prcasting.com

WILMINGTON, NC

- **The Wilmywood Daily** — https://wilmywoodnc.com
- **Cucalorus Film Community** — https://www.cucalorus.org
- **Film Partnership of NC** — https://www.filmnc.org

NEW ORLEANS

- **NOLA Casting** — https://nolacasting.com

- **The New Movement** (improv) — https://www.tnmcomedy.com

ALBUQUERQUE / SANTA FE

- NM Film Office Production Listings — https://nmfilm.com
- Sol Acting Studios — https://www.solacting.com

AUSTIN

- **Austin Film Society** — https://www.austinfilm.org
- **Vicky Boone Casting** — https://vickyboonecasting.com

PITTSBURGH

- **Mosser Casting** — https://mossercasting.com
- **Pittsburgh Filmmakers** — https://www.pfpca.org

NASHVILLE

- **Nashville Acting Studio** — https://www.nashvilleactingstudio.com
- **The Actor's School** — https://www.actorsschoolusa.com

TRADE SECRETS
Loggerheads
REAL TIME ROADMAP TO ACTING
CATHERINE SEWELL

APPENDIX B

ADDITIONAL ADVOCACY AND PLATFORMS

A Nationwide Directory for Training, Casting, Career Development & Industry Insight

ACTOR UNIONS AND PERFORMER ADVOCACY

SAG-AFTRA

The national union representing film, television, commercial, and new-media performers.

Website: https://www.sagaftra.org

SAG-AFTRA FOUNDATION

Free and low-cost education, on-camera labs, voiceover labs, and financial assistance.

Website: https://sagaftra.foundation

FI-CORE CENTRAL

Neutral, factual information about financial-core status for performers.

Website: https://ficorecentral.com

Project Casting – Tips And Advice

Features the differences between union and non-union membership.

Website: https://www.projectcasting.com/blog/tips-and-advice/union-vs-non-union-acting/

CASTING PLATFORMS (PRO SELF-SUBMISSION)

ACTORS ACCESS

Breakdown Services' official self-submission platform; essen-tial for film and TV auditions.

Website: https://actorsaccess.com

Casting Networks

Major platform for commercial, print, and on-camera casting; widely used by agents.

Website: https://www.castingnetworks.com

Casting Frontier

Commercial and digital casting with strong LA/NY presence.

Website: https://www.castingfrontier.com

800 Casting

Regional and national casting platform used heavily in the Southeast and commercial markets.

Website: https://www.800casting.com

BACKGROUND AND ENTRY-LEVEL CASTING

Central Casting

The largest background casting company in the U.S.; entry point for on-set experience.

Website: https://www.centralcasting.com

Casting Calls America Network

Regional casting hubs for indie film, student films, and backgroundwork.

Website: https://www.castingcallsamerica.com

ACTOR TRAINING AND SKILL DEVELOPMENT

Actors Junction Resource Hub

A curated directory of nearly 1,000 actor resources, tools, and training programs.

Website: https://actorsjunction.com

MasterClass (Acting Courses)

Acting instruction from top performers and directors.

Website: https://www.masterclass.com

Improv & Performance Training

The Groundlings: https://www.groundlings.com

UCB (Upright Citizens Brigade): https://ucbcomedy.com

The Second City: https://www.secondcity.com

BUSINESS-OF-ACTING & CAREER STRATEGY

Self-Management for Actors (SMFA)

Career strategy, mindset, and business tools for actors.

Website: https://selfmanagementforactors.com

IMDb Pro

Industry database for research, credits, representation, and production contacts.

Website: https://pro.imdb.com

Stage 32

Networking, education, and industry access for creatives.

Website: https://www.stage32.com

SELF-TAPE, AUDITION AND ON-CAMERA TOOLS

WeAudition

Live readers, coaching, and self-tape support.

Website: https://www.weaudition.com

EcoCast (via Actors Access)

Remote audition system used by casting directors nationwide.

Website: https://actorsaccess.com

SAG-AFTRA Foundation On-Camera Labs

Free self-tape studios and audition labs in LA, NY, and online.

Website: https://sagaftra.foundation/programs

ACTOR SUPPORT, GRANTS & WELLNESS

THE ACTORS FUND (ENTERTAINMENT COMMUNITY FUND)

Financial assistance, housing support, healthcare navigation, and career counseling.

Website: https://entertainmentcommunity.org

INDUSTRY NEWS, PRODUCTION INSIGHT & REGIONAL UPDATES

THE WILMYWOOD DAILY

Wilmington, NC's long-running film community news source; production updates and casting calls.

Website: https://wilmywoodnc.com

DEADLINE

Breaking entertainment industry news.

Website: https://deadline.com

VARIETY

Industry trends, casting updates, and production coverage.

Website: https://variety.com

THE HOLLYWOOD REPORTER

Industry analysis, casting news, and film/TV reporting.

Website: https://www.hollywoodreporter.com

Rachael Leigh Cook
Jonathan Tucker
Agnes Bruckner
Joe Mantegna
Carrie Fisher
and Val Kilmer
"A beautifully acted and directed film with characters that you care about. Very powerful... Thought provoking... Unforgettable!"
- Jan Wahl, SAN FRANCISCO EXAMINER
"One of the most heartfelt depictions of young love in a long time."
- Juan Morales, INTERVIEW
"A drama-packed teen romance! Fine performances by Rachael Leigh Cook and Jonathan Tucker. Agnes Bruckner is magnetic!"
- Karen Durbin, ELLE
Love is a Battlefield
STATESIDE
Based on a True Story

APPENDIX C

UNITED STATES NATIONAL FILM COMMISSIONS

Alabama
https://filmalabama.com

Alaska
https://www.commerce.alaska.gov/web/ded/DEV/FilmOffice

Arizona
https://www.azcommerce.com/film-media/

Arkansas
https://www.arkansas.com/industry-insider/film

California
https://film.ca.gov

Colorado
https://oedit.colorado.gov/film-tv

Connecticut
https://portal.ct.gov/DECD/Content/Film-TV-Digital-Media/Film-TV

Delaware
https://www.visitdelaware.com/industry/film

District of Columbia
https://entertainment.dc.gov

Florida
https://filmflorida.org

Georgia
https://www.georgia.org/industries/film-entertainment

Hawaii
https://filmoffice.hawaii.gov

Idaho
https://commerce.idaho.gov/film-television/

Illinois
https://www2.illinois.gov/dceo/whyillinois/Film

Indiana
https://www.iedc.in.gov/industries/film-media

Iowa
https://www.iowaeda.com/film/

Kansas
https://www.kansascommerce.gov/program/creative-arts-industries/film/

Kentucky
https://filmoffice.ky.gov

Louisiana
https://louisianaentertainment.gov

Maine
https://www.maine.gov/decd/film

Maryland
https://marylandfilm.org

Massachusetts
https://mafilm.org

Michigan
https://www.michiganbusiness.org/industries/film-and-digital-media/

Minnesota
https://www.mnfilmtv.org

Mississippi
https://filmmississippi.org

Missouri
https://mofilm.org

Montana
https://montanafilm.com

Nebraska
https://film.nebraska.gov

Nevada
https://nevadafilm.com

New Hampshire
https://nh.gov/film

New Jersey
https://www.nj.gov/state/njfilm/

New Mexico
https://nmfilm.com

New York
https://esd.ny.gov/industries/tv

North Carolina
https://www.filmnc.com

North Dakota
https://ndtourism.com/industry/film

Ohio
https://ohiofilmoffice.com

Oklahoma
https://okfilmmusic.org

Oregon
https://oregonfilm.org

Pennsylvania
https://dced.pa.gov/film

Rhode Island
https://film.ri.gov

South Carolina
https://www.filmsc.com

South Dakota
https://sdvisit.com/film

Tennessee
https://tnentertainment.com

Texas
https://gov.texas.gov/film

Utah
https://film.utah.gov

Vermont
https://filmvermont.com

Virginia
https://www.film.virginia.org

Washington
https://www.washingtonfilmworks.org

West Virginia
https://wvfilm.com

Wisconsin
https://wedc.org/program/film/

Wyoming
https://www.filmwyoming.com

"Life isn't about finding yourself; it's about creating yourself.
So live the life you imagined."
—Henry Thoreau
Trade Secrets
by
Catherine Sewell
Releasing 2026
www.donnaink.shop
www.donnaink.net
CATHERINE SEWELL
TRADE SECRETS

"Hitch your wagon to a star."
—Ralph Waldo Emerson
Trade Secrets
by
Catherine Sewell
Releasing 2026
www.donnaink.shop
www.donnaink.net
CATHERINE SEWELL
TRADE SECRETS

APPENDIX D

ADDITIONAL RESOURCES FOR ACTORS

Professional development, craft expansion, and industry literacy.

- **Actor Marketing & Branding Tools** - These help Actors build a professional presence beyond head-shots and reels.
    - **Canva (Branding & Actor One-Sheets)** - Easy templates for actor one-sheets, social media branding, and pitch materials. **Website**: https://www.canva.com
    - **Linktree (Link Hub for Casting Profiles)** - A single link to house Actors Access, Casting Networks, reels, and social media. **Website**: https://linktr.ee
    - **Beacons (Portfolio-Style Actor Landing Pages)** - A more polished alternative to Linktree for actors. **Website**: https://beacons.ai
- **Voiceover & Audio Tools** - Even on-camera actors benefit from VO skills.
    - **Voices.com** - Marketplace for voiceover auditions. **Website**: https://www.voices.com
    - **Voice123** - Professional VO platform with strong indie and commercial opportunities. **Website**: https://voice123.com

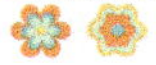

    - **Audacity (Free Audio Editing) -** Perfect for VO practice, self-tapes, and ADR. **Website**: https://www.audacityteam.org

- **Script, Scene, and Rehearsal Tools - Scriptation -** Industry-standard script annotation app used on film / TV sets. **Website:** https://scriptation.com

    - **Rehearsal Pro -** Line-learning and scene-study app used by working actors. **Website**: https://rehearsal.pro

    - **ColdRead -** AI reader for practicing scenes when a partner isn't available. **Website**: https://coldreadapp.com

- **Actor Financial & Business Literacy -** Actors are small businesses — these tools help them operate like one.

    - **QuickBooks Self-Employed -** Tracks mileage, expenses, and quarterly taxes. **Website**: https://quickbooks.intuit.com/self-employed

    - **Mint or Rocket Money -** Budgeting tools for actors managing inconsistent income. **Websites**: https://www.mint.com / https://www.rocketmoney.com

    - **Entertainment Community Fund Financial Wellness Workshops -** Free financial education for performers. **Website**: https://entertainmentcommunity.org

- **Mental Health & Wellness for Performers** - Acting is emotionally demanding — these resources support resilience.

    - **Backline (Mental Health for Creatives) -** Free support groups and wellness resources for entertainment professionals. **Website**: https://backline.care

    - **The Loveland Foundation -** Therapy support, especially for BIPOC creatives. **Website**: https://thelovelandfoundation.org

   - **Insight Timer** - Meditation app widely used by actors for grounding before auditions. **Website**: https://insighttimer.com

- **Industry Education & Career Literacy** - Actors who understand the business work more consistently.
   - **No Film School** - Free education on filmmaking, production, and set culture. **Website**: https://nofilmschool.com
   - **IndieWire** - Industry news with a focus on independent film. **Website**: https://indiewire.com
   - **Film Courage** (YouTube) - Interviews with actors, directors, and casting professionals. **Website**: https://www.youtube.com/user/filmcourage
- Networking & **Community Platforms**
   - **Women in Film (WIF)** Chapters nationwide supporting women and nonbinary creatives. **Website**: https://womeninfilm.org
   - **Film Fatales** - Community for women and nonbinary directors — great for actors seeking collaborators. **Website**: https://www.filmfatales.org
   - **Meetup (Local Actor Groups)** - Search "acting," "improv," "film," or "screenwriting" in your region. **Website**: https://www.meetup.com
- **Actor-Friendly Film Festivals & Showcases** - Great for networking, exposure, and learning.
   - **Sundance Collab** - Workshops, labs, and online classes for emerging creatives. **Website**: https://collab.sundance.org
   - **Austin Film Festival (AFF)** - Known for its writer-actor-director networking culture. **Website:** https://austinfilmfestival.com

- **Cucalorus (Wilmington, NC)** - Actor-friendly, community-driven festival. **Website**: https://www.cucalorus.org

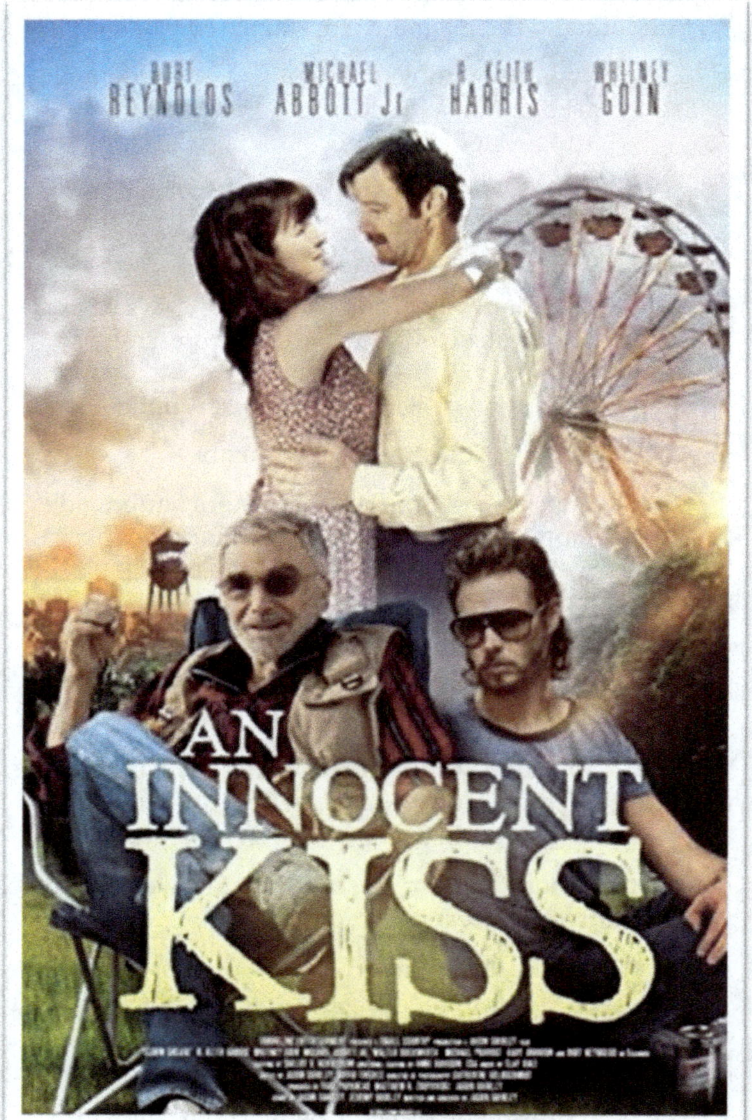

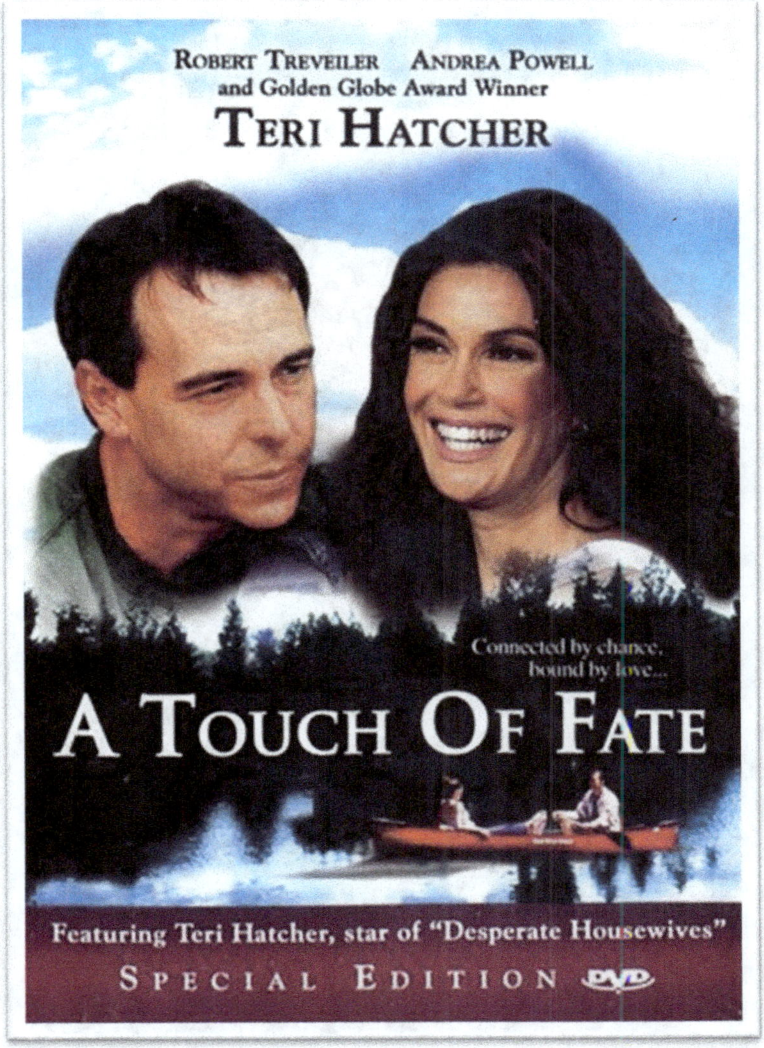

ROBERT TREVEILER ANDREA POWELL
and Golden Globe Award Winner
TERI HATCHER
Connected by chance,
bound by love...
A TOUCH OF FATE
Featuring Teri Hatcher, star of "Desperate Housewives"
SPECIAL EDITION DVD

Colin
FIRTH
Ellen
BURSTYN
Patricia
CLARKSON
with Amber
TAMBLYN
and Orlando
BLOOM
MAIN ST.

HAPPILY
NEVER
AFTER

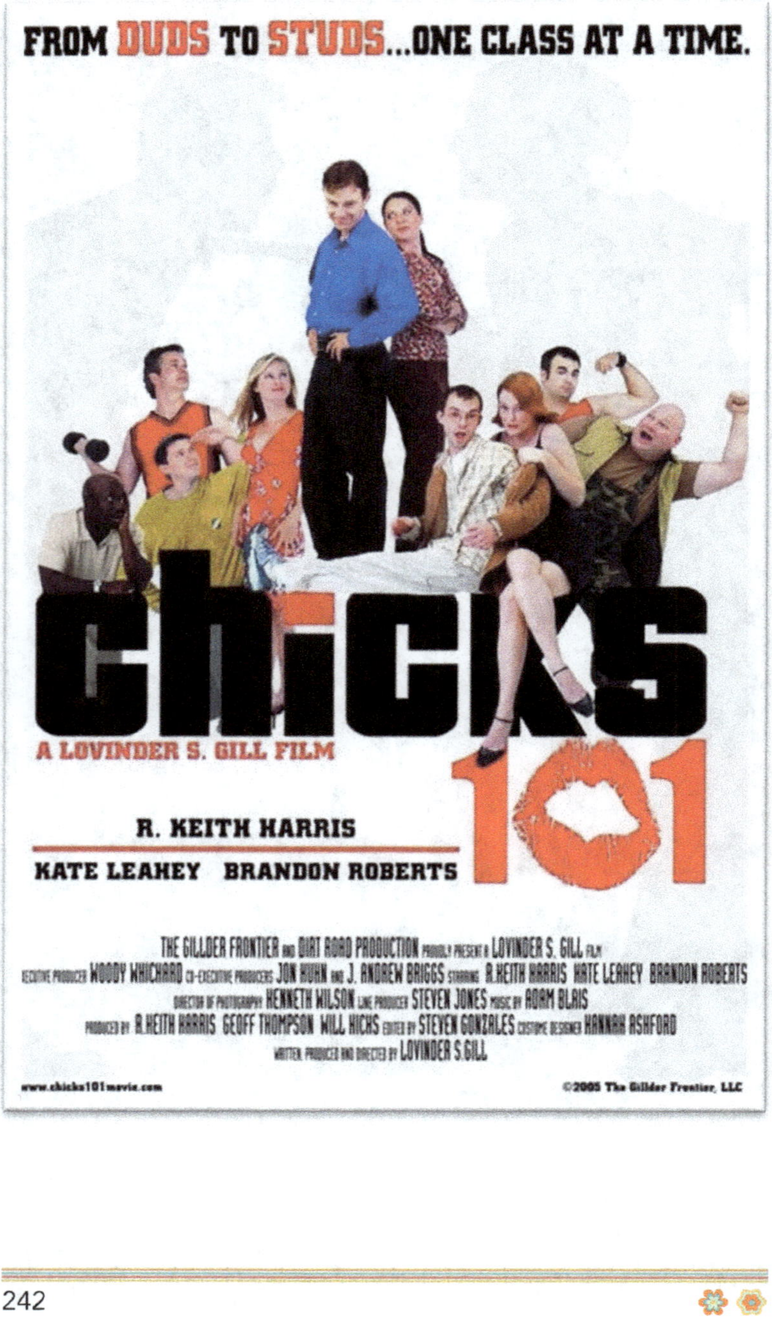

FROM DUDS TO STUDS...ONE CLASS AT A TIME.

CHICKS 101

A LOVINDER S. GILL FILM

R. KEITH HARRIS

KATE LEAHEY BRANDON ROBERTS

THE GILLDER FRONTIER DIRT ROAD PRODUCTION LOVINDER S. GILL
WOODY WHICHARD JON HUHN J. ANDREW BRIGGS R. KEITH HARRIS KATE LEAHEY BRANDON ROBERTS
KENNETH WILSON STEVEN JONES ADAM BLAIS
R. KEITH HARRIS GEOFF THOMPSON WILL HICKS STEVEN GONZALES HANNAH ASHFORD
LOVINDER S. GILL

www.chicks101movie.com

©2005 The Gillder Frontier, LLC

TRADE SECRETS: Real-Time Roadmap To Acting
Published by *DonnaInk Publications*
Brandywine, Maryland
www.donnaink.net
msdonnalquesinberry@donnaink.net

Editorial preparation, interior layout,
and typography were completed by *DonnaInk Publications*.
Cover design and visual composition were developed in collaboration
with the *DonnaInk Design Studio* and Author Catherine Sewell.

www.ingramcontent.com/pod-product-compliance
Lightning Source LLC
LaVergne TN
LVHW020051110826
845155LV00021B/61

9781939425317